Love Notes 2

Love Notes 2

The Journey Of Love

Lola Campbell Brown

Illustrations by Mark Brown
Photos by Tracey Hopkins and Colin Campbell

authorHOUSE®

AuthorHouse™
1663 Liberty Drive
Bloomington, IN 47403
www.authorhouse.com
Phone: 1-800-839-8640

Published by AuthorHouse   01/18/2013

ISBN: 978-1-4817-8096-4 (sc)
ISBN: 978-1-4817-8097-1 (e)

Any people depicted in stock imagery provided by Thinkstock are models, and such images are being used for illustrative purposes only.
Certain stock imagery © Thinkstock.

This book is printed on acid-free paper.

Because of the dynamic nature of the Internet, any web addresses or links contained in this book may have changed since publication and may no longer be valid. The views expressed in this work are solely those of the author and do not necessarily reflect the views of the publisher, and the publisher hereby disclaims any responsibility for them.

Contents

Reflections on April

Reflections on May

Reflections On June

Reflections on July

Reflections on December

Acknowledgments

I wish to thank Tracy Hopkins. Tracy thank you for all your help for your photographs and the time you spent helping me to format everything. I am most grateful to you.

Thank you Mark you are truly talented and a credit to us all

Thank you to all my friends who encouraged me.

Angela, Pamela, Chidi, Trevor, Yvonne, Sheila, Wendy and Paul.

Thank you O'neil and Micah for your patience

Finally, Auntie Al I am indebted and full of appreciation for all the help and assistance you gave me. I love you so much!

Foreword

Approximately a year ago, Lola Campbell-Brown, having completed her first book, *LOVE NOTES*, for publication, was excitedly looking forward to writing her next, *LOVE NOTES 2 The Journey of Love*. Having listened to her ideas for this second publication, this member of her audience felt impressed that the finished product would be very interesting. One was not to be disappointed.

The first book, *LOVE NOTES,* comprises a treasure of quotes, short verses and poems celebrating love. This second book does the same *and far more*. It takes the reader on an interesting journey through the months of the year—each with its brief history, poignant images and connected anecdotes. The work ends with a series of love poems, verses and quotes.

With this expanded scope, *LOVE NOTES 2* explores the pursuit of fulfilling one's dream and vision through self-awareness, the extracting of lessons from and for life, the consequent regulating of oneself, and positives to be derived from good relational alliances. All this is presented by way of a unique mix comprising a summary historical archive on the months of the year, a number of anecdotal experiences, sets of motivational directives, and a good measure of touching poetry—all for one's aesthetic indulgence, general education, or self-help.

Campbell-Brown's lyrical style of writing and her use of fitting symbolism have resulted in a work of art that is vibrant, interesting and easily understood. In a powerful way, it is potentially positively life-changing; hence one would not hesitate to recommend this work.

It is universally relevant to all who have a dream or vision to be realized, and to all who love, have loved, will love, or would be loved.

Aldred L. Walters

My Journey of Love

The Customs and practices surrounding love and marriage was different in ancient times. Marriages were frequently arranged and people did not always marry for love. Yet, in the Bible, love and relationship issues were at the heart of most incidents. Love is mentioned no fewer than 458 times in the Old Testament and more if deutromological accounts are included.

There are many lessons that may be extracted from our loving encounters which is why it is such a popular subject, and widely addressed in most cultures. Importantly, what we may perceive as negative experiences may become life lessons which provide essential personal development which we can use to build our characters. This in itself provides learning which we can then share to provide emotional enrichment.

My encounters of love have been both diverse and spurious, sometimes I have defined love incorrectly, my perceptions tainted with misdiagnosis. I have been known to lack the boldness to act on feelings and convictions, missing out on new possibilities. However, I am certain that true love is active, visible, and should be demonstrated unreservedly.

Along my journey of love, one of the most defining moments was when I learnt that in order to love others appropriately, I needed to cultivate and develop healthy love for myself. In doing this we are moulding ourselves towards love and will eventually make healthier investments in others. Wholeness and love for us takes time to develop. Our innermost being must manifest self-love, not selfishness, and display the characterisation of loving habits. We should continuously speak to ourselves raising our inner consciousness so we may display the unique gift we are to humanity, and share the gift that we are, so, others will benefit.

I hope 'Love Notes2 the Journey of Love' will take you on your own journey of self-realisation becoming an 'Aid Memoir' to implementing your vision and following your own dreams. Love is a language that is understood by all, to be loved is a blessing, but, to pass on the love you have for yourself to someone else is an even bigger blessing and is an indulgence that should not be missed.

God bless you and happy reading!

January's flower the Carnation

New days
Dawning,
Shadows disappearing,
Warm sunlight appearing,
Daylight nearing,
You delight in new vision,
Give thanks for acquisition,
For you know your commission,
And see your provision

Lola Campbell-Brown
2012

Reflections of January

January

New Beginnings, Entrances, Doors and Gateways and Endings

January acquired its name in 700BC from a roman emperor called King Numa Pompillus. Its meaning and symbolism comes from Roman mythology. January's Latin, name is _Ianuarius_ and is named after 'Janus', specifically 'who according to legend, was the Roman god of beginnings, endings, doorways, entrances, gates and gateways. Depending on your source of reference, Janus may be depicted as a two headed god because he was said to have the ability to turn one face to reflect upon the past and another face freshly pointed upon the future. The word 'janitor' is derived from Janus. During the same year it replaced March as the first month of the year.

January is also known for the commemoration of Epiphany, also known as, **'Three Kings' Day or 'Theophany.** In several Christian traditions, Epiphany is commemorated as the time when God revealed His only begotten son to the world, the beginning of a new covenant of love between God and humanity and the climax of the Christmas or advent season. A celebratory feast is held on January 6th or slightly later on January 19th, if using an eastern calendar.

The revelation of the divine Son of God was said to bring hope, vision, and light to a world that was steeped in sinful darkness. The days to Epiphany are usually counted from the evening of

December 25th until the morning of January 6th, which is the Twelfth Day. In following this older custom of counting the days beginning at sundown, the evening of January 5th is the **Twelfth Night**. In some cultures this is a highly festive season and traditions include the baking of a special **King's Cake**.

"Help me to see clearly the pathway of love that was designed for my being, that I may attract goodness to my person and light to my affairs."

Reviewing Your Vision
January 1st-7th

The beginning of the year is a good time to develop insight and to review where you are in terms of your life's journey. Traditions aside, have you ever considered what January means to you? Is it a time of reflection when you make resolutions, or a time of renewal and review, incorporating your experiences over the last year? Who knows, you may have your own Epiphany and the doors of opportunity may swing open, giving you entrance and birth to a myriad of new things that will help you engage and re-kindle your vision.

The word epiphany Introduced to us earlier may be applied more generally to describe experiences of an instantaneous nature. These experiences may be a manifested understanding of a concept, or the comprehension of a perceived reality by a sudden, intuitive, spiritual realisation that is more personal to you. You may bring yourself to an epiphanic experience when you make the sudden connection and realisation of your destiny and vocation.

Reflection is a powerful tool when practised regularly, and is useful in structuring thoughts when making decisions. Social Work practitioners are encouraged to reflect on their practice. This process is viewed as a professional competence, and is used in risk assessments and complex casework. There is certainly no harm in pressing the pause button intermittently, withdrawing from a fast paced modern society, to gather one's thoughts. Reflection helps us to construct the best atmosphere to configure plans, to execute our vision and dreams. I was always fascinated by the word 'Selah' often 'written in the verses of the Psalms in the Bible, it means to 'pause and reflect'. Selahs are quite common in meditative styles of worship encouraging focus and intuitive reflection, usually on the themes raised in the Psalm.

Re-Kindling Your Vision
January 8th-14th

You may consider taking all or some of the following actions to ensure that Selah's are incorporated during your day, to measure your progress regarding the development of your dream and vision:

❖ keep a journal or diary where you can write little notes to yourself to record actions and steps you intend to take to rekindle your vision and to record your reflection for learning.

❖ Make some time at the beginning or end of the day to record the notes in your journal. You will be giving yourself space to reflect.

❖ Ask yourself a series of questions to help you focus on your vision. Try the following suggestions:

- What should I be doing now?
- What hopes and dreams do I have for the year ahead?
- Are there any smaller tasks which may act as stepping stones to a larger dream?
- What stage am I in my life's journey?
- What is my overall vision for the future?

❖ Write down your vision and display it in a place where you will see it every day.

❖ Once a day repeat your vision a loud to remind yourself of it.

❖ Get an empty photo frame and write key words or find a picture and put it in the empty frame.

Congratulations, you have taken steps to re-kindle your vision and progress your dreams.

There's a voice that speaks inside of you
It's a voice that's strong and clear.
Directs your path, and bids you do.
The voice that gives you steer.
It's your inner voice that leads you on,
With courage strength and sight.
Your spirit voice that sooths your soul
To encourage and bring light.
It's your voice of inner love that speaks
At darkest times you'll see,
To say and bring you out of things
It speaks to set you free.

Discovering, Defining, and Using Your Inner Voice
January 15-22nd

Once you have reacquainted yourself with your vision and your connections have been made, the next step to take is to seek ways to affirm your vision or dream. The affirming process does not constitute one single action, and you may need to implement a course of repeated actions to ensure effectiveness, and so you discover which methods will work for you. You will need to think about how you will embed your dream or vision in your mind, in order to visualise the success of your plans. One of the ways you can do this is by discovering your inner voice.

Everyone has an inner voice and there are many ways to extract and discover it. My definition of the inner voice is drawn and connected to my Christian Faith. I recognise that there are a variety of ways in which we can find our inner voice but wish to make clear the origin of my personal belief system.

Defining Your Inner Voice

The inner voice may be defined as the articulation of the spirit, the inner person. The inner person is strengthened by the Holy Spirit who influences, guides behaviour, comforts, and is a resource offering partnership, particularly in times of difficulty.

A further and interesting definition is offered by Douglas Bloch. In his book 'Listening to your Inner Voice' He states:

"The inner voice is *that source of wisdom that lies within us*"

Your Inner voice will help you to explain experiences you have to yourself.

My belief is that we all have an inner voice which has to be located and activated. It is the inner voice that strengthens us and invokes self-belief. This is paramount if you are alone and do not have the support of loved ones, or an embracing community. Our inner resources come into play and act as our reserve drive to give us energy and impetus to fulfil our life's dreams.

Using Your Inner Voice

"Everyone who wills can hear the inner voice. It is within everyone."

Mahatma Gandhi.

There are many ways in which we may use our inner voice. I have learnt many lessons from the stories of King David in the Bible, but, one in particular comes to mind in 1Samuel Chapter 30. David and his soldiers arrived at the town of Ziklag where they had set up camp. David and his troops had returned from another town where they had been victorious. Not killing anyone, the Amalekites attacked and raided Ziklag and burned it down, taking everyone hostage.

David and his soldiers grieved at the loss of their loved ones. On seeing the devastation of their temporary home, they broke down and cried. This experience was enough to send them over the edge. They wept so much that they used up all their tears. The men began to turn on David making him the scapegoat, blaming him for all that had happened. It is so disheartening to know that men who had just been victorious in one battle were now victims of another.

King David found himself in an extremely difficult position, isolated and alone. Many leaders have found themselves in similar circumstances, they are successful in one project and unsuccessful in another. Their understudies or congregants are excited and then angry. The leaders are fine when they are doing what everyone wants but are not so popular when leaders whistle blow or discipline. They are then blamed for the failure of that company or church. David responds uniquely. Using his faith he turns to his inner resources for strength. The King James version of the Bible passage states that

"David encouraged himself in the Lord" We also know that David wrote a Psalm relating to this incident which is Psalm 42. In verse 5 David questions himself stating:

> "Why art thou sad, O my soul? and why dost thou trouble me? Hope in God, for I will still give praise to Him : the salvation of my countenance,"

This is a classic demonstration of using the inner voice when challenged. David uses his inner voice and through rhetorical questioning encourages himself at a time when he is alone and in need of comfort. When he has no allies he gains strength from this action and regains his composure to lead and manage a frustrated, grieving and angry group of men.

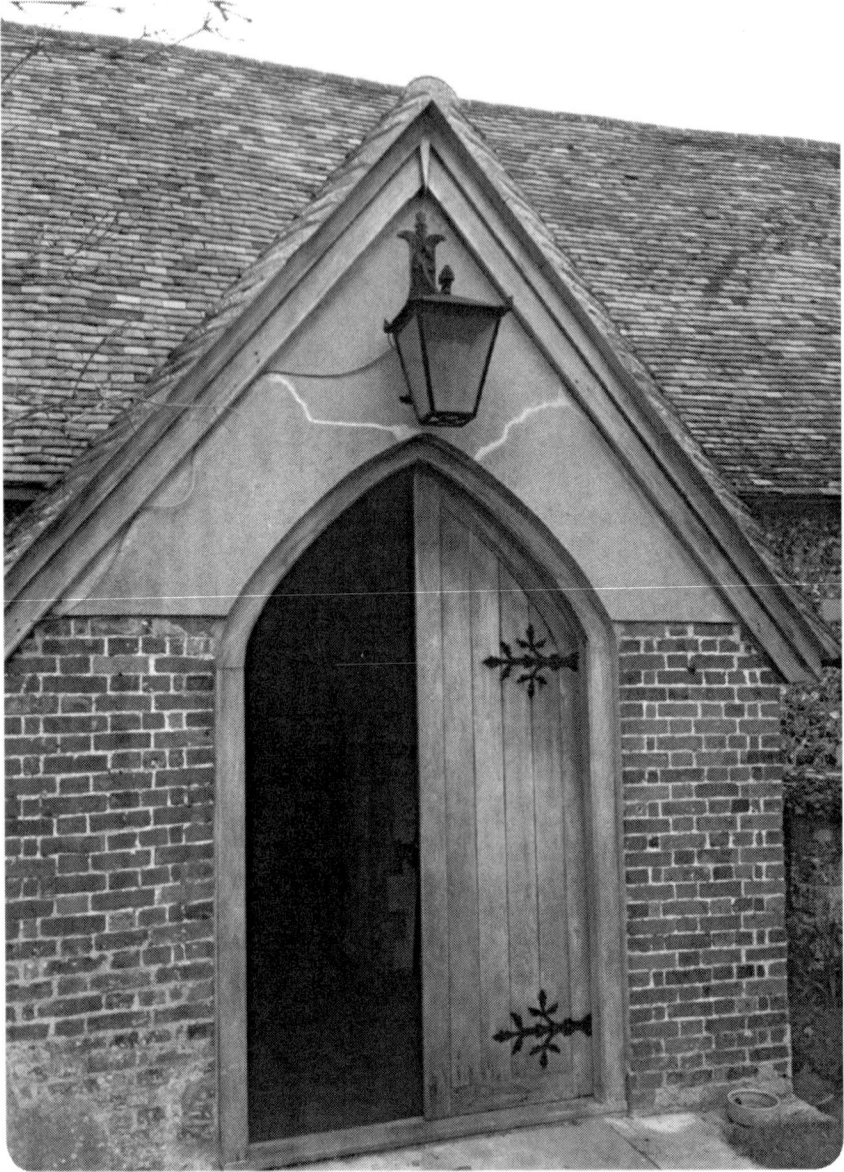

Over time, most people develop an inner voice but are not always aware of it. The inner voice may be strongest when we are faced with challenges, doubts or fears. There will be times when you are implementing your vision or dream that you feel discouraged and unsupported. This is when you will need to draw on your inner resources, encouraging yourself regardless of faith, gathering strength and momentum to continue following your dream and implementing your vision.

Seven Ways to use your Inner Voice

- To sort out doubts and concerns
  Sort them into those you can readily address and those that need further attention. Listen to your doubts and concerns, and question yourself as to their validity.
- For action planning, writing it down if necessary.
- Use your inner voice as a "sounding board" for problem solving. You may discover alternatives and solutions or come to the realisation that you need outside help.
- To proactively deal with challenges. Ask yourself when additional clarification may be in order, or if there are any issues you may have overlooked. Have you had any similar challenges and was your response ever effective.
- Warning you about danger
- For self-encouragement and affirmation.
- For keeping in touch with your spirit and soul.

Fine Tuning Your Inner voice
January 23ʳᵈ-31ˢᵗ

We previously discussed locating, activating, and using our inner voice. Now, what we must do is sharpen our instrument and fine tune it so that it functions appropriately when needed. Fine tuning our inner voice will help us prepare for hardships, difficulties, and eventualities. King David in the Bible used his inner voice for self-encouragement when he was in a very difficult situation. When life becomes stressful or distressing we can be tempted to do what David's soldiers did, scapegoating, blaming, or taking it out on someone else. My mum defines this attitude in a simple phrase she used when I was growing up, "Misery loves company". It is always easy in a crisis to blame someone else and not to recognise where the fault really lies. The temptation to have what I call a pity party, is a trap many of us fall into. Affirming our vision in a crisis is important so the challenges we face do not get the better of us. We must gather strength and momentum to keep our focus on the right things.

There have been times in my life when I have not been as fit as I have wanted to be. I have had to enrol myself on gym programmes, and incorporate exercise in my daily routine. Rebuilding my fitness level was never easy because I unsurprisingly fell into bad habits. These had to be broken fairly early on in the process, which I found hard, realising I had to be consistent. Sometimes the exercises actually hurt and it took sheer will power to continue with the regime. Diet was also an important consideration. I had to make sure I was eating the right foods to get the correct nutrients for my fitness plan so my body would function correctly.

Fine tuning our inner voice is comparable to getting ourselves physically fit. We need to feed ourselves correctly with the nutrients that will nourish our inner person so our inner voice can respond appropriately and speak accurately.

So, how do we fine tune our inner instrument making sure it is fit for purpose?

1. **Use positive affirmations to encourage yourself**—I went through a phase when I was unhappy with my physical appearance. I used a bible quotation, Psalms 137. There is a magnificent verse where David, who wrote this Psalm, states that he is wonderfully and fearfully made.

   Biblical Psalms may not be everyone's cup of tea, but find appropriate resources that suit you, and ones which will build your confidence. Don't be afraid to vocalise the words. There is something very special about the spoken word, you will be encouraged, your confidence will be built, and you will be reminded about what you are trying to achieve.

2. **Be very careful about what you say**—We may not realise that our words are containers of creative power. Proverbs chapter 18v 21 in the Bible states that "the power of life and death is in the tongue". You can give birth to or kill your dream, just by what you say. Be mindful about who you share your vision and dream with.

Some people may not understand your dream or vision so will try and discourage you. Be selective and only share your thoughts with people of like mind, It is also sad to say that you will meet some people who are envious of you, particularly if you have obvious talents be selective about what you share.

3. **Keep Good Company**—Be careful about the kind of company you keep. Try and associate with people who will encourage you. Speak to people who are successful. Get yourself a coach or mentor if necessary. It is advisable to mix with people who are like-minded, who have achieved.

4. **Do your research**—Find out as much as you can about your area of interest, joining networks if necessary.

5. **Help Others**—We are all at different stages of our life's journey, helping someone along the way is similar to making a viable investment. Mentor and coach others, it will help you in your journey.

Reflections on
February

February

From Latin Februium: meaning purification

The word February originates from the Latin word Februarius, and februare meaning to "purify" or "expiate." It is the second month of the year and the shortest. The Romans had a purification festival, sometimes called the festival of forgiveness on February 15th every year, and great festivities were held to restore the empire's focus on morality and righteous living.

February was used as an occasion to ask for forgiveness of sins from their deity, and to forgive anyone who had wronged them. The idea of devoting an entire month to purity, morality, and forgiveness sounds quite refreshing. It was a time of peace making, reconciliation and restitution.

February is also known for hosting 'Valentine's Day' The famous saint of Love. Valentine's Day is celebrated in many countries around the world, mainly in the West. It has never been a public holiday, but, this has never hindered any celebration. Historical aspects of Valentine's Day—remain a mystery—. February has a long tradition of being associated with romance, and Valentine's Day, in its present form today, is a residue of both Christian and primeval Roman tradition.

The Catholic Church recognizes at least three different saints named Valentine or Valentinus, all of whom were martyred. One legend contends that Valentine was a priest who served during the third century in Rome. When Emperor Claudius II decided that single men made better soldiers than those with wives and families, he outlawed marriage for young men.

Valentine, realizing the injustice of the decree, defied Claudius and continued to perform marriages for young lovers in secret. When Valentine's actions were discovered, Claudius ordered that he be put to death. Other stories suggest that Valentine may have been killed for attempting to help Christians escape harsh Roman prisons, where they were often beaten and tortured. Others say that Valentine fell in love himself and was ill fated because of this.

Originally, "St. Valentine" was a liturgical celebration. This celebration was deleted from the General Roman Calendar of saints in 1969 by Pope Paul VI.

As well as purity, February symbolises sacrifice and service. It is the beginning of Lent in Christian traditions—a period before Easter when the forty days that Jesus fasted is commemorated. This time of sacrifice, penitence, fasting, prayer, and reflection, is usually a time to consider the less fortunate and disadvantaged. Some churches refer to this practice as a 'Lent Call', or 'Act of Service'. This tradition involves showing kindness to others in a practical way, genuinely demonstrating Christian love.

Forgive For You
February 1st-13th

A change of month or season is always a good time to reflect on your life's journey and to evaluate how well you are doing with your goal setting. Are you still following your dream or vision? Are you keeping up with the commitments to make them into a reality? You may become more aware of what adjustments you need to make to keep track of your dream and vision.

How will you use the month of February to progress your dream and vision? February was a time of peace making and forgivness for the Romans. I believe that prolonged unforgiveness is unhealthy and causes much discontent. Harbouring any amount of ill feeling and bitterness should be actively discouraged, as it can impact very negatively on physical health which can be fatal for some of us. What a way to end one's life! Unforgivness and bitterness drains us and consumes a lot of energy unecessarily. It is best to let things go, keep our minds clear, and maintain a focus.

The Process of Forgiveness

It is helpful to understand forgiveness as a process and not to conceptualise it as a one of act. It can be a difficult pathway for most of us and yet for Christians, forgiveness is a principal tennet of the christian faith. Mistakenly, the forgiveness process is often short-circuited when issues are not fully addressed. The guilt of our percieved unforgivness can also cause paralysis, preventing us from moving forward. Bitterness, unforgiveness, or unresolved issues can hamper the progression of a vision or dream. I suspect that the Romans instituted the festival of forgiveness because they knew it would instill health and clarity of mind, aswell as restore focus, peace and stability. This knowledge may have contributed to why they had a powerful dynasty and reign. Forgiveness takes time and we should allow ourselves to fully engage in the process.

Useful Tips For Engaging in The Process of Forgiveness

1. Own up to how you feel about the situation or incident.

   Reflect, and make sure you can talk about what happened. Speak to a trusted person if you can, but make sure it is somone who is responsible enough not to break your confidence or use the information against you.

2. Keep the wound Clean!

   This is the title of a sermon I have yet to preach. Metaphorically speaking, we need to keep our wounds clean or infections and all kinds of nasties may set in. Planning a revengful attack is not an appropriate response and will not alleviate any pain we may be experiencing; all it may lead to is, emotional combustion and negativity making you unfit for purpose.

3. Forgiveness is a sacrifice.

4. Recognise that Forgiveness is for you!

Look after youself and do what you have to do to allow yourself to forgive. Choose methods that suit you and not anyone else.

5. Forgiveness does not necessarily mean reconciliation.

    We should aim to find peace and resolution within ourselves. This does not always mean reconciliation with the one who has hurt us or that we condone what has happened.

6. Change Your Perspective

    Learn to forgive and forgive to learn. Forgiveness helps to heal our hurt feelings and we should aim to change our perspective to extrapolate the learning we can from the situation, so, rather than being a victim we are victors.

7. Put your energy into looking for alternatives.

    Try different ways to get your positive goals met rather than through the experience that has hurt you. Instead of mentally replaying your hurt, seek out new ways to get what you want. Try out new forums and situations.

8. Remember that a life well lived is your best revenge. Instead of focusing on your wounded feelings, and thereby giving the person who caused you pain power over you, learn to look for the love, beauty and kindness around you. Forgiveness is about personal power.

9. Forgivness is a Sign of Maturity

10. Amend your story of grievance to remind yourself of your heroic choice to forgive. This will empower you.

Keep a balance, but do sow seeds of kindness to others. Forgive those who have hurt and try not to hold on to any bitterness as this will zap your energy and cause you to lose focus on what you have to do. The seeds you sow will return to you and you may receive a sacrifice or service that you really need from someone else. February: reflect, forgive and move on recognising that **Forgiveness is for YOU!**

Living waters ripple, running deep, penetrating the soul and spirit giving life to dry bones, satisfying the thirst of love.

Loving Yourself
February 14th-28/29th

"I do not trust people who don't love themselves and yet tell me, 'I love you.' There is an African saying which is: Be careful when a naked person offers you a shirt."

—Maya Angelou

Earlier, we learnt that the word February means 'to purify' or 'expiate' and I believe that true love brings with it innocence and purity. The month of February hosts Valentine's Day on the 14th when people with romantic feelings for a particular person may send that person cards, gifts and text messages. Popular gifts include chocolates and flowers. In the United Kingdom (UK) it is the tradition to send your gift or card anonymously).

Valentine's day has an interesting and varied history, with elements of paganism and Christianity. Originally, It was part of the Catholic liturgical calendar but was taken out by Pope John Paul V1 in 1969.

The day first became associated with romantic love in the circle of Geoffrey Chaucer in the High Middle Ages, when the tradition of courtly love flourished. It had evolved into an occasion in which lovers expressed their love for each other, by the 15th century.

I am a firm believer in not waiting around for romantic love. Before we can truly say that we love anyone, we really need to love ourselves. Mayo Angelou is clear in her statement above that she is dubious about anyone who expresses love yet cannot love themselves appropriately.

Why is self-love so important?

1. You cannot give what you haven't got!

   We radiate what is on the inside of us. If all we have inside is self-hate then hate, rather than love is what will be manifested.

The fresh and living waters of pure love will never run dry but will continuously spring up into a charitable oasis of eternal love!

2. Self-love helps you to create a life that you love!

   Anything that is not developed on a firm foundation of self-love will eventually crumble. Self-love gives an infrastructure to develop skills and learning that will help to propel you forward and assist you in procuring a sturdy value system.

3. Healthy self-love should not be confused with selfishness!

   Self-love should not be confused with an unhealthy disregard for others. Self-love is really about the unconditional acceptance of oneself, and does not preclude the love we have for other people. In fact, by displaying healthy love for ourselves we can actually show others how much we love them. For example, a mother should love herself enough so she is strong and healthy to care for her children. Her physical and emotional wellbeing will be transmitted from her to her loved ones.

4. Like attracts like!

   Love on the inside will attract love on the outside. Like attracts like! As we love ourselves we radiate love to others. For those of us who need partners, we will only attract negativity if we do not learn to love ourselves. When we love ourselves we will attract positive influences which affect our lives in affirming ways.

5. Self-love nourishes the soul and feeds the Spirit.

    For our own emotional and spiritual health, we should cultivate self-love. This is therapeutic to our inner self and helps to preserve our mental state, comforting our soul and continuously lifting our spirit. Even the Bible advises that Husbands should love their wives the way they love themselves. Imagine how dangerous this would be if a husband hates himself, no love would be given at all.

6. Self-love means having a good relationship with yourself.

    Self-love means total acceptance of oneself and you will not beat yourself up unnecessarily over your human flaws.

    On the next Valentine's Day do something for yourself to show 'you' that you love 'you'. After all, you are worth it. I am not saying that you should not celebrate the day with a loved one, but there are times we should give one's self a healthy love injection, ensuring our inner love immune system is still working.

The song "Greatest Love of All," written by Michael Masser and Linda Creed (performed by Whitney Houston) encapsulates it all for me, because if we believe in God or a higher being the following lyrics are appropriate, "I found the greatest love of all Inside of me".

Reflections of March

March

Until~700BC March was the start of the year and the beginning of the war season. The Saxons called the month *Hreth-monath* after their goddess Hreth. The month is also identified with the Greek god, Ares, their war god equivalent.

March originates from early Roman times and is named after Mars, the Roman god of war. (Martius) Other historical names for March include *Maaliskuu* in Finnish, meaning earthly month. It was called this because during maaliskuu, the ground was finally visible from under the snow. The Saxon word Lentmonat is named after the equinox and gradual lengthening of days. This became the eventual root-name for Lent.

March is now the first month of spring in the Northern Hemisphere. The numbered year began in March in Russia until the end of the 15th century. Britain and its colonies continued to use March 25 until 1752, when the UK fully adopted the Gregorian calendar. Many other cultures and religions still celebrate the beginning of the New Year in March and historically it has kept the start of the military campaign for the recruitment of new soldiers! This practice has past and present significance. Firstly, Mars was said to be the son of Juno and Jupiter and second only to his father in veneration of Roman soldiers; it seemed appropriate therefore to recruit soldiers in a month named after the god of war. Secondly, Rome's climate is Mediterranean, making March the ideal month to not only welcome in the spring season, but also to start the recruitment of soldiers for the military.

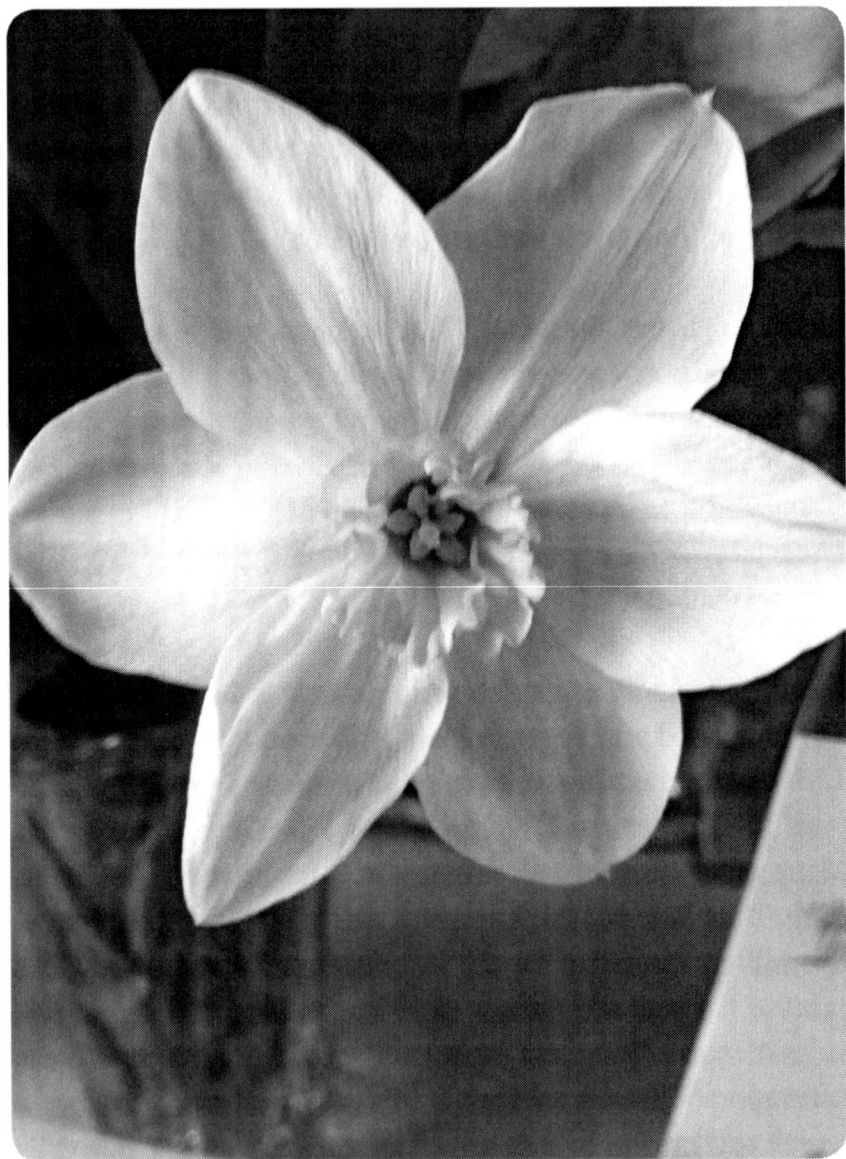

Spring Clean your Mind
March 1ˢᵗ-13ᵗʰ

In the West, there is a tradition that is practised called "Spring Cleaning". It is the act of thoroughly cleaning your home at the end of winter. I must admit to indulging in this practice, and I tell myself that the beginning of March, when spring is upon me, is a great time to make a clean sweep of things.

I have never just practised a tradition for the sake of it: there always has to be some practical significance for me. In the case of spring cleaning, I find that springtime is when I am inspired to take on a new project, to learn a new skill, or to make a significant change in my life. The budding of new leaves and flowers seem to encourage change in me. I find Spring-time so welcoming and this leads to inspiration.

From time to time I watch a television programme called 'Hoarders', the programme is about people who compulsively hoard things. Some cannot even live in their homes, because the space has been taken over by all the things they have hoarded over time. It is quite evident that most of the hoarders are trying hard to hide themselves behind their hoards. They are affected mentally, and show an imbalance in their lives, within which hoarding is symptomatic of their unhealthy mental state.

I suppose, in a way, when I spring clean, it is symbolic of me clearing my head and making space in my life for new things. I commenced this book project during springtime and it has been thoroughly exciting and enjoyable.

When we are working towards our dream and implementing a vision we should periodically, spring clean our minds, making ourselves less prone to distractions, so as not to lose our focus. Spring-cleaning our minds can help us to clear emotional debris giving us the full propensity to work towards our dream. The following are ways we can do this:

Give yourself a Break

Take a few minutes each day to pray (if this is your belief), meditate and reflect on your life. Gratefulness for everything, can change your perspective and influence the way you handle challenges and your approach to life generally.

Release negativity:

Most people have to make the effort and make the choice to be happy. Happiness doesn't just happen. You have control over your thoughts, not the reverse. You are responsible for cultivating the frame of mind that brings about happiness and contentment.

Rest: Even God rested!

Even if you do not believe in God, common sense tells us we should rest. Most of us are tempted to stay up later during the summer because of the longer days. I have been guilty of this, and I have had to discipline myself to go to bed on time, so I can rejuvenate and be fresh for my daily life assignments. We all have a responsibility to take care of ourselves by ensuring that we get enough sleep. Our bodies need the time to regain its energy.

Make a new Friend:

Nurturing friendships is an integral part of our happiness. Studies have proven that people with strong friendships live a lot longer. I also believe that people come into our lives for a purpose. With the right people around us we fulfil our dreams a lot quicker.

Spring-cleaning your mind does take time and effort, but the rewards and advantages are great, bringing about peace of mind and holistic wellbeing.

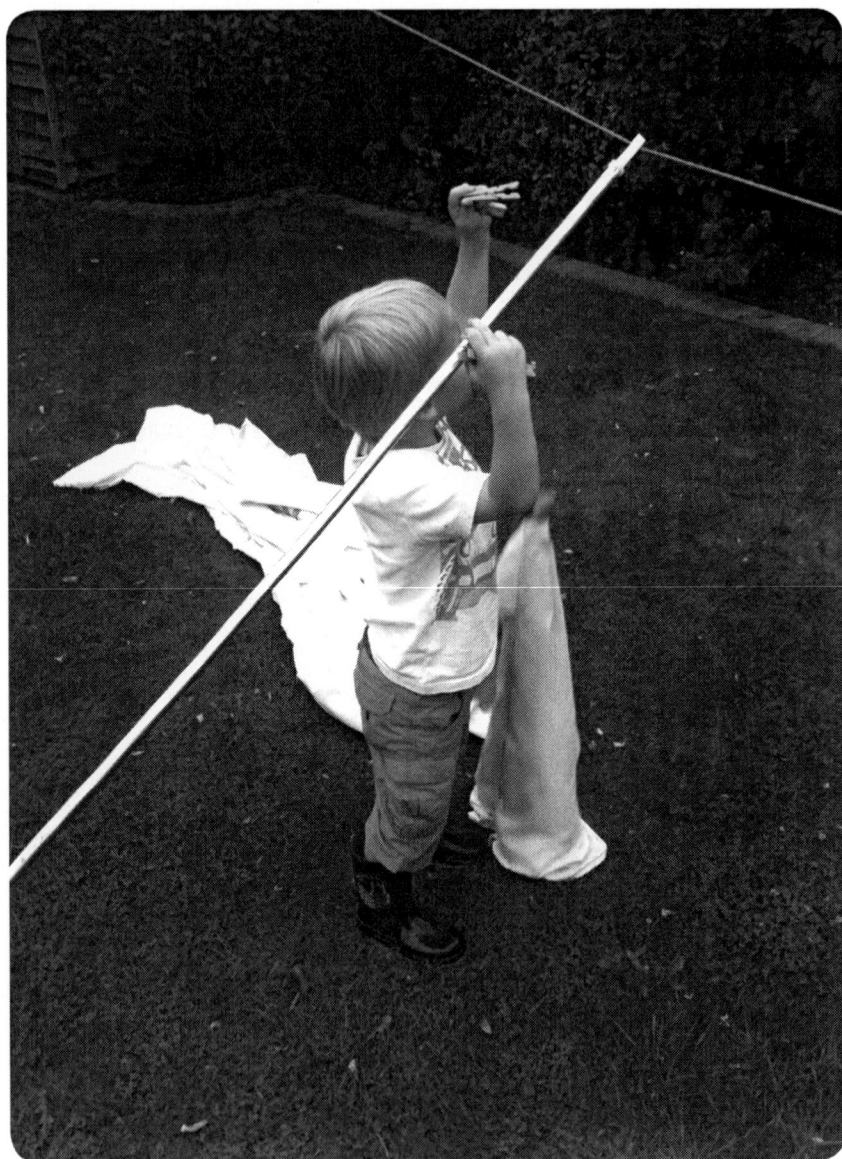

Knowing which battles to fight
March 14th-21st

During our lifetime we will face many challenges and opportunities to become upset, defensive, and unsettled. My belief is that these things happen mainly to distract and prevent us from fulfilling our life's destiny and they are usually time consuming, energy zapping, creativity killing intruders.

A biblical proverb states that: "avoiding a fight is a mark of honour; only fools insist on quarrelling".

We need to be discerning enough to fight the battles that really matter and not bother about the less important ones. By making this decision and taking this action you will command peace and tranquillity in your life. I have been far more effective when I have chosen my battles wisely. Winning the battles that are truly important gives you more credibility and respect. Dr Richard Carlson, author states in one of his best-selling books, "Don't sweat the small stuff" that:

> **"When you fight or argue over every confrontation, people will perceive you as a confrontational troublemaker. If you challenge only those issues that are truly and personally offensive to you, your opinions and disagreement will bear more weight, and people will listen. You will also be keeping track of what is truly relevant to you."**

I totally agree with Carson. When you are following a dream or vision you do not want to spend all your time fighting everything; it will take you away from your primary goal, drain you, and cause you to lose track of your dream. A prominent pastor friend's mum would always say this as he was growing up:

"He who chooses his fights well, will live to fight another day"

What his mother is really saying is that we should choose to fight significant battles so we may conserve our energy to address issues that *are more meaningful. We should never allow ourselves to be judged because we chose not to fight a certain battle; something much bigger may come up where we will need all the strength we can muster. C. Joybell, says this:*

"Choose your battles wisely. After all, life isn't measured by how many times you stood up to fight. It's measured by your ability to make the best of what life has to offer."

This is a fair point! By choosing your battles wisely you are maximising your resources, and not drawing on your precious reserves. There will be times whilst pursuing you dream that you will have to be strong because there will be challenges and times of discouragement. Fighting senseless battles will unnerve you and take you off-course.

I will end with this truthful quote by Dale Carnegie:

> **"Any fool can criticize, complain, condemn, and most fools do. Picking your battles is impressive and fighting them fairly is essential."**

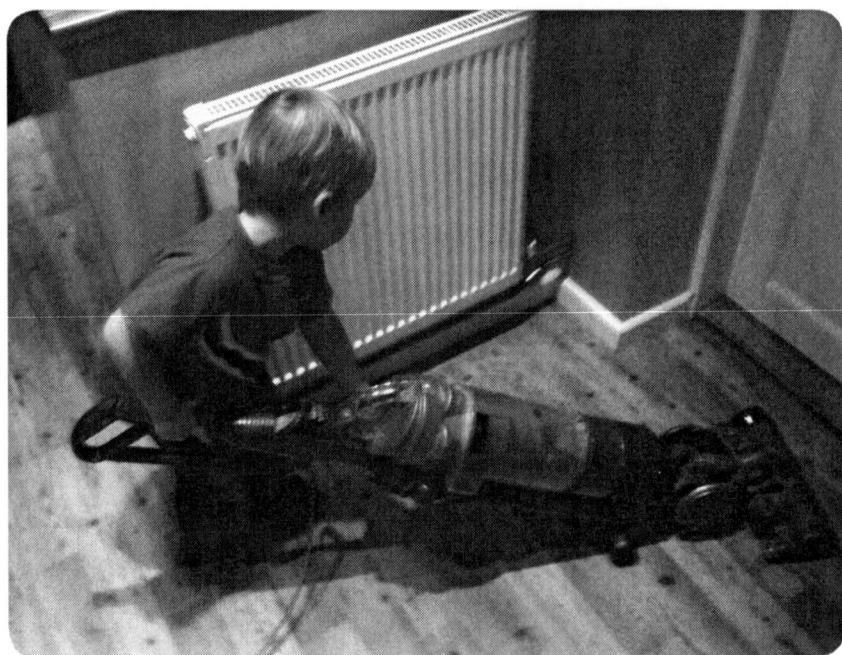

Make your mind up in March
March 22nd-31st

Have you ever had to deal with unpredictable weather conditions?

The season of March is often unpredictable; British weather is like this at the best of times. One never knows whether it will be warm, sunshine or rain and so it is difficult to know what clothes to wear . . . And what crops should be planted in the garden. As a result of this, there have been times when I have been over-dressed, under-dressed, too warm, become wet and dishevelled due to ill preparation. However, in following your dream or vision, it is important to pre-empt conditions that will affect your mind-set and spirit. In times of unpredictability it is a good discipline to learn new skills or to improve our areas of development. In many of the roles I've had, giving effective presentations has been important. To do them more effectively I had to learn a particular programme on the computer. During the summer vacation, I enrolled on a specific computer course to understand this particular programme. This made my presentations look more professional and I learnt several shortcuts, which saved me a huge amount of time. As a result of this, I was even confident when presenting.

Springtime is not only known for weather unpredictability, but it is known as a time of change. We can see the changes happening before us: the days become lighter, the birds start singing and a number of animals prepare themselves for nesting.

It is a time of great conception-the trees are budding-flowers are appearing—Everything 'springs' into action.

When we implement a vision or dream, it is important to activate our minds and nurture our emotions so we can spring into growth, to challenge unpredictable eventualities.

Why not, therefore, pre-empt some of these challenges by

- Learning a new skill
- Begin networking to make new contacts
- Get yourself a mentor or coach to propel you forward and to help crystallise some of your ideas.

In other words—'Spring' yourself into action! This will help you to go forward ensuring you are some way towards implementing your dream and vision.

Reflections on April

"Illuminate my pathway that as my light transmits to others, I and all will benefit from my shining spirit of love."

April the Open Month

Over the years there has been much controversy as to the origins of the word April but, one of the most common explanations is that it derives from the Latin and this traditional etymological root suggest that April originates from the Latin word 'aperire', "to open," drawing on the analogy to it being the season when trees and flowers begin to "open".

This explanation is also supported comparatively with the Modern Greek use of the term' νοιξις or (anoixis)'opening' for spring.

It has been suggested that April was named in honour of the goddess Venus (Roman) and Aphrodite being the Greek equivalent. In the latter years April is more commonly known as Aphrodite's month, the goddess of love, beauty, pleasure and procreation. Legend has it that Aphrodite was attended by the Three Graces, Charm, Beauty and Joy and is often represented by a dolphin, dove, or swan. She came into being when Cranus castrated his father Uranus and threw his genitals into the sea. They began to churn and bubble and from the sea foam (or aphros) came Aphrodite, born as an adult.

The Anglo-Saxons called April *Oster-monath* or *Eostur-monath*. It is said that this is where our word 'Easter' comes from. Being the fourth month of the year in both the Gregorian and Roman calendars, April is one of four months that has thirty days. It was added to the Roman calendar just before January and February by King Numa Pompilius in approximately 700 BC.

April Showers
April 1ˢᵗ-13ᵗʰ

In Ancient Egypt the land was dependant on the river Nile for its irrigation, and as the water inundated the soil, it gained nutrients so crops could grow, which in turn would provide food for the Egyptians. The Egyptians were also able to raise their livestock providing another source of food. As a result, towns developed and Egypt became a strong economic power.

In many Christian traditions water symbolises refreshing, cleansing and growth because it is essential to life. Metaphorically, it is also used to symbolise the Word of God. It is believed that God's word is essential for life and sustenance. The Word of God, is refreshing, causes purity, and growth in one's life. Water metaphors are used throughout the Bible, from Genesis to Revelation.

When I think of April I am nearly always reminded of April showers, which is why my mind ventured towards water metaphors. Rain is a frequent occurrence in British weather. As the saying goes, 'April showers bring May flowers'.

The symbolism regarding water may be used in this instance once again. There is the suggestion that after showers of rain the fruitful results will be the appearance of flowers in the month of May. We may draw an interesting life analogy from this and appreciate that there are times when we will endure periods of discomfort because we can see a fruitful end and our prize will be the fruitful end product.

Joyce Meyer, a prominent Christian minister, uses an interesting phrase to summarise this notion; she says, "We will have beauty for ashes". The trade off for enduring difficult circumstances is that growth; productivity, strength, beauty and fruitfulness will be the end result.

Rain can also be a metaphor for blessings. Throughout the Bible rain has signified blessings and abundance. The analogy of inundation is drawn from the fact that in the same way the river Nile inundated the land of Egypt, our lives may be inundated by blessings from above.

In some communities rain is venerated because it is seen as promoting growth and land fertility, and so, it is never taken for granted particularly in places prone to drought.

So you see, April showers may depict several things. Who knows? April might become your month of love and beauty and you may reap a rewarding end product! Make the best of it, and remember you won't always be uncomfortably wet. Start drying yourself off looking forward to your May flowers; reap your fruitful prize.

Come Into Bloom
April 14ᵗʰ-21ˢᵗ

Spring flowers come along and usually cheer me up after I have survived what I feel are long winter months. The flowers seem to appear when I most need them and I am almost excited in seeing the first blooms of what I call April gladness.

We learnt earlier that April comes from the Latin word 'aperire', to open, and is linked to the opening of spring. When I think of openings, I always think about opportunities and making use of them. Openings come to us when we least expect them, but when they appear we should maximise the "openings" presented to us.

Recently I went to a conference for leaders in the community. Honestly speaking, I did not really want to go because it meant giving up a weekend. I had been working for a number of weekends in my main employment. However I decided to go. It turned out to be one of the best decisions I made, because I met like-minded people. We also formed a network with contacts that keep in touch and encourage one another. More importantly, the people I met helped me to come into bloom, by helping me to see things in a different way. Development was also reciprocal: I contributed to others as they contributed to me. I came away from that conference a different person, which resulted in me developing different strategies, a variety of approaches to work, making new contacts, initiating new projects. I started to shine once again, the long and short of it was that I came into bloom and it was noticeable.

For one to come into bloom the conditions need to be right. Sometimes we have to create the right conditions for ourselves, tilling the ground, putting the correct nutrients in our lives, making full use of the soils that are around us, or finding or discovering it within ourselves. Aren't flowers beautiful when they come into bloom? Their fragrance and beauty overwhelming? What is less known is that coming into bloom requires a great deal of hard work and we must be prepared to cultivate ourselves so we may bloom when the time is right. Help yourself to come in to bloom.

Picking your flowers
April 22ⁿᵈ-30ᵗʰ

I am told by reliable sources that the best time to pick most flowers is when they are in bud or half open. You will then see the flowers slowly open and their colours and petals will start to show. The buds may not open if the flowers are picked too tightly. Tulips and roses are vulnerable to this so great care should be taken when they are plucked.

It is not advisable to pick flowers in the middle of the day because that is when the sun is at its hottest and the heat tends to lower the water content in the stems shortening the flower's lifespan. One should also be mindful of rain: wet flowers should be shaken gently to remove the excess water. Too much water will damage flowers—especially the delicately petaled ones. Ideally, the best time to pick your flowers is early morning when flower stems are filled with water after the cool night air. You may pick them after sun down too, but one should be mindful that sugar reserves in the stems are at their highest in the mornings.

When we start to implement our vision or dream we need to choose our moments and be strategic about how we do things. I once attended a management course and the Organisational Coach talked about the three principles of strategic thinking:

- Knowing
  - o First of all, one needs to accumulate knowledge to gain a firm understanding of an area that is being developed. With regards to the implementation of vision or dream, its best to find out everything that we can about the areas that we want to progress. Wisdom is the implementation of this knowledge.

- Thinking
  - o Your mind-set is really important, we have to be open enough to learn and be flexible enough to work differently and to try a variety of approaches. It is also important to understand the way you learn, so that you retain new learning more appropriately.

- Behaving
  - o A Change in mind-set should influence our behaviour and once we have implemented the new learning, that change in behaviour is usually evident to all and most of all-ourselves.

Strategic implementation of one's vision or dream means that we must Know, think, and behave accordingly!

Reflections on May

May

The most widely accepted explanation of how the month of May was named was that it was called May after **Maia**, the Roman goddess of spring and growth. The name *Maia* relates to a Latin word which means' increase or growth'. According to the early Roman calendar, May was the third month. Later, the ancient Romans used January 1ˢᵗ for the beginning of their year, and May became the fifth month. May has always had 31 days.

The first day of the month of May is known as *May Day.* Although summer does not officially begin until June, May Day, historically, marks the beginning of summer. May Day celebrations have been carried out in England for over 2000 years and different counties mark it in their own special way. The Romans celebrated the festival of Flora, goddess of fruit and flowers, which marked the beginning of summer. It was held annually from April 28th to May 3rd.

The month of May is also said to invoke joy, romance and love and it is customary in a range of cultures to celebrate the entrance of summer with exuberance and joyous expressions because May is the time of year when we begin to experience warmer weather. The blossoming trees and the colourful flowers are on display all around us. Temperatures are warm, but not hot; and by now we usually say goodbye to the ice and snow. Gardeners are busy planting their vegetables; birds and animals are preparing for new life and there is the vibrant buzz of new life; everywhere.

Lola Campbell Brown

Mother's Day takes place on the second Sunday of May in America and the Caribbean. The first Mother's Day in 1908, was a commemoration of new life among humanity. The first celebration was recognized by the president and congress and officially became a holiday in 1914.

Make the month of May a meaningful time for you. A time when suddenly everything blooms, you shine and come into your own or have new revelations or new growth. Whatever the month means to you, you should make the best of every situation.

It's Getting Hot

May 1ˢᵗ-13ᵗʰ

May is the time in the northern hemisphere, when the weather changes and usually warmer weather begins. The benefits of the waters of April can be seen by the appearance of flowers.

Unfortunately, flowers are not the only things that appear in warmer weather. A few years ago I was in my small city garden in the south eastern part of London. I by no means had a large space, but the ground was extremely fertile. I grew all kinds of vegetables and herbs and used the produce to fundraise for different charitable projects.

It was extremely humid that year and we were experiencing very hot weather from as early as April. My garden was rather over—grown and two friends came round to help restore order. As we sawed through the unruly shrubs, something green and black slithered away. My friend shouted," Are you scared of snakes?" I flew inside the house like a shot and refused to go back into the garden, fearing I would see other snakes. It was only a harmless grass snake. Nevertheless, it was a snake.

We have all encountered periods in our lives when things are 'hot'; meaning, that we are facing a range of challenges at the same time and maybe we are fearful regarding some of the confrontations. My snake challenge had me running scared and I had to make several adjustments so my fears were alleviated. I kept the plant areas but removed most of the grass and I made sure it was kept low in the places it remained.

Ron Kenoly, a renowned Christian worship leader, wrote these lyrics in his song entitled 'Go Ahead': "If you catch hell don't hold it/ if you're going through hell don't stop."

Choose Your Fuel Wisely
May 14ᵗʰ-21ˢᵗ

I grew up cooking with gas cookers, so when I had to use an electric cooker at college I must confess that I did not cope very well.

In my culture we are quite ritualistic when cooking our chickens. Every hair or feather has to be singed. (We do this even if the butcher has already done it)

Gas cookers have open flames so it can be easily done. It is much harder to do this on an electric cooker because rather than having an open flame the cookers contain rings, so of course, you cannot burn the hairs or feathers.

I really had trouble adjusting and for years I suffered with what I call, 'Not prepared properly Chicken syndrome'. I had to learn ways round it, but when I was in control of choosing my own cooker, I understood and knew why I wanted a gas cooker because I knew what I wanted it for and had clarity regarding its purpose.

One has to know what they want and know why they want it. When you are implementing your dream and vision, be clear about why you are doing something, what the purpose is, and why you need to do it.

Gaining clarity for yourself will help you not to waste time and energy on fruitless projects that will stagnate you rather than help you move forward.

Choose your projects wisely; this will enable you to conserve your much needed energy for the things that you have to do, and get right.

Gauge the Heat
May 22nd-31st

When I am cooking certain dishes it is important that I get the right temperature. The other day a friend of mine was cooking what we call fried dumplings, (a Caribbean snack usually eaten for breakfast). The fire was way too high, so the oil over-heated and the dumpling was burned on the outside but raw on the inside.

Her only option was to throw away the entire batch of burnt, raw snacks and start again. She was furious with me, but more furious with herself because I had told her several times to turn the fire down, but as she knew best she didn't want to listen and so, during the process of her burnt offerings I kept quiet, avoiding the 'burning' of her tongue.

This incident teaches an important lesson; it is crucial to gauge the temperature and heat when cooking, because if you don't, you'll end up with food that is both unpalatable and inedible. Additionally, you would have wasted valuable time.

There are times in life when we have to gauge the heat, and instinctively know when we are about to get burnt. This will help us to take evasive action where necessary. We can then make sure we are in the right place at the right time, ensuring the conditions are correct for what we are attempting to do.

When implementing your dream or vision, test the waters so you don't end up doing what my friend had to do, throwing away something valuable and having to start from scratch, once again.

There is an old Chinese proverb, which states; "Only fools never learn from other peoples mistakes." Learn from what has happened before and make sure that you can pre-empt situations so that we won't be in a position of being burnt and left raw with hurt on the inside.

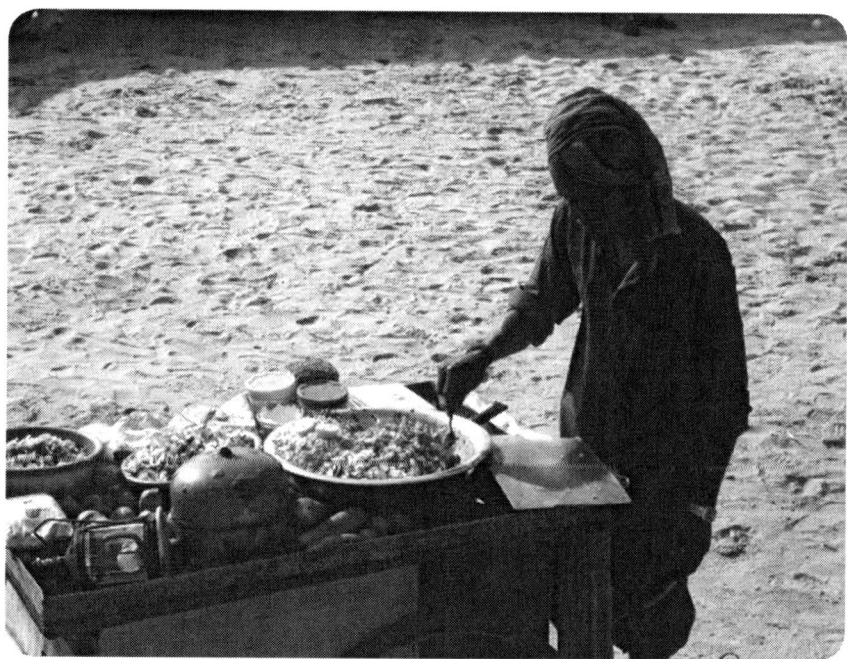

Reflections On June

June (Juno's Month)

The Gregorian calendar is used over most of the world today and June is its sixth month. In the Roman calendar, June was considered the fourth month and had only 29 days. Julius Caesar gave the month 30 days in 46 B.C., when he reformed the Roman calendar.

June is named after *Juno* who is the principal goddess of the Roman Pantheon. She is the goddess of marriage and the well-being of women and is the wife and sister of Jupiter. She is identified with the Greek goddess Hera.

The name comes from the Latin word *iuniores,* meaning "younger ones".

According to Bede, **June** was known to the Anglo Saxons as **Ærra Liða.** 'He defines *"Litha or Liða"* as 'gentle' or 'navigable', because in both June and July the winds are gentle making the seas more navigable and calmer for sailing. Most Scholars agree Bede's definition is sound because the adjective *liðe* appears regularly in other Anglo-Saxon contexts with the same meaning, along with the verb *liðan* meaning 'to sail'.

June is the month with the longest daylight hours of the year in the Northern Hemisphere and the shortest daylight hours of the year in the Southern Hemisphere. Winter begins during June in the Southern Hemisphere, and it brings with it cold, rainy weather in that region. In the Northern Hemisphere, spring ends, and summer begins. It is the time when the flowers are beautiful. It is especially known for being the month when roses bloom and has often been referred to as the' Rose Month.

A Rose Among Thorns
June 1st-13th

Growing through Adversity

I would not call myself the world's greatest gardener but I have been quite successful in growing roses. I've learnt several things whilst on my rose quest. One is that you need to choose the right Rose for the space you have, they require a great deal of sunlight or they won't thrive, they also need to be watered regularly and systematically. Once these basic needs are met they often grow without much trouble. It is important to prune rose bushes to a third of their original size after they have finished flowering. Even though it may feel brutal, healthy growth will be encouraged for the following year.

The fact that these beautiful flowers often grow amongst thorns is something that has always fascinated me, hence the phrase" a rose among thorns." I was often pricked as a child trying to pick beautiful roses, which were growing, in the area I lived. I wondered why such aromatic flowers had to be surrounded by these spiky and piercing barbs. One theory is that thorns actually protect the sweet rose from its herbivore predators. In order for the tender rose to live out its life span, you may be pricked by their guardian prickles.

Another analogy may be drawn from our rose scenario, which is, regardless of harsh circumstances, or adverse or challenging events, one can still shine and be successful. When we begin to follow a dream or implement a vision we will inevitably have challenges. Thorns represent challenges. Have you noticed that for every perfect rose there are several thorns surrounding it? Somehow the rose manages to grow and looks as beautiful as ever through these thorns.

In order to follow our dreams successfully we should be prepared to grow through adversity. This can mean many things. Thorns can signify difficult people who don't believe in your gift or talent and who discourage you from following your dream. If you encounter this, like the rose you have to be single-minded even if the thorns are on your very stem, meaning that you are surrounded by negativity, and the discouragement may even come from family members or close friends. Try to learn from the experience so that you may grow and gain strength to continue on your journey. Don't stop for too long merely licking your wounds. Rest if you must to gather your strength, cleaning your wounds, lest infection should set in.

We should be mindful that thorns have a dual role: they may be painful prickles, or protective guardians. Challenges are opportunities we should make use of. They help us to become more creative, aid our development and increase our strength for the next bout. To learn and grow in times of adversity is a choice we can all make. We can bloom like the rose!

Sailing on Calm Waters
June 14ᵗʰ-21ˢᵗ

The Anglo Saxons called June *Ærra Liða* meaning navigable. Sailing was the primary mode of transport and it was a blessing not to have to navigate harsh seas which were life threatening and treacherous.

I am not a very good sailor. I tend to get very seasick. One day whilst in the Caribbean, I booked a boat trip. It would be a luxurious way of observing the magnificent coastline and the transparent viridian sea. It was quite choppy going out and although I wasn't ill, my stomach felt very unsettled. I concentrated so much on my feelings of nausea that I didn't get to appreciate the breath-taking views, the wild life or anything else. I did however learn an important lesson, which was that I could have prepared myself a lot better than I did. By taking a travel sickness tablet and not eating any rich foods immediately before, I would have minimised feelings of seasickness. Then there was my mind-set. I should have focused on the surroundings which were absolutely breath—taking. This should have taken my mind off the nausea. Eventually, we reached calmer waters. I was able to join in all the planned activities: eat, drink, and socialise.

For some, stormy waters mean fear and danger where they cannot function. For others, storms bring about illness, pain and incapacitation. On the contrary, calmer water is like respite for some. They can indulge in activities that they would not otherwise have the capacity for. Calm waters are an opportunity not to be missed, bringing clarity and tranquillity to body and mind. When there is calm we should make use of the time so that we may give our bodies respite from the rat race.

A Midsummer Delight

June 21st-30th

I once attended a wedding in Mid-June. The church service was held in a lovely church in one of the suburbs on the outskirts of London. It was one of those places where you could mistakenly think you were in the heart of the countryside but realistically you were only a few miles from the city of London.

Unusually, for a British wedding the reception was held outside, with no shelter or a marquee in sight. If you have ever experienced the randomness of British weather, then you will understand why I say It was an unusual occurrence.

The day turned out to be unbelievably beautiful. The sun shone; there was a cool breeze which took the edge off the summer heat. The guests mingled in the pretty gardens of manicured lawns and hedges; freestyle cottage areas with sweet smelling herbs attracted each guest. I noticed a display of unusual roses and allium flowers, so stunningly eye catching with their globe like appearance. I learnt later, that they were actually a variety of flowering onion. Strawberries and Loganberries were out in abundance too, and a shrub with marigold—like flowers was also in full bloom. It was all so magnificent and very splendid indeed.

I came to an important realisation at the wedding: I had been so busy complaining about the unpredictability of British weather that I had never really taken the time to enjoy and reflect on the wonderful midsummer days that we had, even if they were few and far between. My complaining and moaning had deterred me from recognising and enjoying something that was uniquely special that I could tap into and undeniably appreciate. I believe I could have stunted my own growth by focusing so much on the negative, not allowing myself to extrapolate the positive from even a dire situation. I had to remind myself about how important it is to have the right mind set in order to advance and move forward.

When one wants to progress a vision or dream it is not helpful just to only see the negatives in a situation. We should try and look for positives even if they seem few. There may be learning that we may extract for our own good. Develop an attitude of gratefulness; this helps us to regain our composure and position of power in a negative situation.

I am really grateful for my friends who, against all the odds, triumphed over our British weather and took the risk. They overcame negativity and gave themselves and their friends a gorgeous celebratory event for all to remember on a wonderful and special midsummer's delightful day!

Reflections on July

July—
Julius Caesar's Month

Julius Caesar reformed the Roman calendar in 46 BC. In the process, he renamed July, after himself. July is spelt *Julie* in Middle English and comes from the Latin, *Julius mensis* meaning, month of Julius.

Julius Caesar is the first person to give his name to an entire month. However, he was careful not to take a month that was already claimed by one of the Roman gods, such as June named for the queen of the gods, or March named for Mars, the god of war. He changed the name of **Quintilis** (meaning fifth month) to **July. Quintilis** had been the fifth month prior to 153 B.C when the new year was moved from the 15th of March to 1st January. July has remained stable as months go. It has always possessed 31 days.

In the Southern Hemisphere July is a winter month, but, it is usually the hottest month of the year in the Northern Hemisphere. During July, when there isn't much rain, the grass often loses its greenness. Some flowers are plentiful in July, because they strive on the heat. Insects are usually in abundance!

In the Catholic faith the month of July is dedicated to the Precious Blood of Jesus. The entire month falls within the liturgical season of 'Ordinary Time', which is represented by the liturgical colour green. This symbol of hope is the colour of the sprouting seed and signifies in the faithful the hope of reaping the eternal harvest of heaven, especially the hope of a glorious resurrection.

July is special to me as it t is the month when I was born. I celebrate my uniqueness and am grateful that I have lived another year. In July I celebrate with Family and friends expressing my gratefulness for having them around.

July the Water Lily Month
July 1ˢᵗ-13ᵗʰ

If you are bit of a botanist then you will know that *Nymphaea* is the scientist's name for **water lilies**, which are considered to be jewels of the pond kingdom because of their natural beauty and purpose. Water lilies are often spread across pond waters giving colour and visibility and serving an important purpose by contributing to the eco-system. They control the growth of algae, keep the pond and the creatures in it safe and healthy, and do a great deal to maintain the well being of the pond environment.

Water Lilies provide shade that cools the water in the summer months and as July is one of the hottest months of the year in the Northern Hemisphere, water lilies play an important role in this respect. Their shade also gives shelter from the sun to any fish, giving respite from the many predators that may be lurking around. The flowers absorb nutrients in the water that would normally feed objectionable green algae, keeping the pond clear and giving the appearance of cleanliness. I love water generally, but, the sound of running water relaxes me, and a pond filled with lilies is definitely an added bonus.

Like the water lily, we are gorgeous, purposeful, individuals put on earth to fulfil needs that are crucial. We should see ourselves as gifts adding value to our communities, and change agents affecting our environments positively. How we visualise ourselves is important to procure success in whatever project we embark on. We are beautiful and gifted, and are required to play our part to reach our destiny and fulfil our dreams in this life. When we are in our rightful place we will aspire to what we ought to be. We will shine and our purpose will certainly become known.

Regeneration & Growth
July 14ᵗʰ-21ˢᵗ

As I said previously, in the Catholic faith, the month of July is dedicated to The Precious Blood of Jesus. The entire month falls within the liturgical season of Ordinary Time, which is represented by the liturgical colour green. This symbol of hope is the colour of the sprouting seed and arouses in the faithful the hope of reaping the eternal harvest of heaven, especially the hope of a glorious resurrection. It is used in the offices and Masses of Ordinary Time. The last portion of the liturgical year represents the time of our journey to heaven, pressing onward for our eternal reward.

I am quite partial to the month of July because it is my birth month. It is usually hot in the northern hemisphere and a time when crops planted in the spring are maturing and growing. The crops usually reach their peak but are dependent upon summer rains to grow and to survive the summer heat.

July's summer days provide us with opportunities to engage in activities that we perhaps would not otherwise attempt during winter, and the Sun, may inspire us in different ways, to do a variety of things. I tend to travel more in July, locally and abroad. I have gained so much during my explorations of new cultures; it has expanded my learning and challenged my thinking in a number of ways.

When opportunities present themselves we should make use of them, as procrastination is one of the biggest killers of dreams and visions. When we make use of opportunities we can begin to grow, redevelop and regenerate, particularly if we approach things with an open mind. Christians believe that Jesus' death and resurrection can transform our lives, giving us the impetus to see and to live life in a completely different way. Let the month of July be a month when you can be energised, renewed, and regenerated to progress your dream.

Water your dream with encouragement; and regenerate your vision with new learning: you will begin to live a transformed life.

Going for Gold
July 22nd-31st

It is impossible to know the exact date that humans first began to mine gold, but the graves of the necropolis were built between 4200 and 4700 BC, indicating that gold mining could be at least 7000 years old.

The process of producing gold can be divided into six main phases:

- Finding the gold
- Creating access to the gold
- Removing the ore by mining or breaking it up
- Transporting the broken material from the mining face to treatment plants
- Processing
- Refining

A number of different techniques can be used to mine gold. I had the opportunity in the 1980s and 1990s to spend time in South Africa where gold mining has a long history. The three most common methods used there are panning, open cast and shaft mining.

1. Panning

Panning is customarily a manual technique that is used to sort gold from other sediments. Wide, shallow pans are filled with sand and gravel (often from river beds) that may contain gold. Water is added and the pans are shaken so that the gold is separated from the rock and other materials. Because gold is much more dense, it settles to the bottom of the pan.

2. Open cast mining

This is a form of surface mining. Surface layers of rock and sediments are removed so that the deeper gold rich layers can be reached. This type of mining is not suitable if the gold is buried very deep below the surface.

3. Shaft mining

In South Africa the gold reefs are thin and slope at an angle underground making some deposits awkwardly deep and difficult to reach. Shaft mining is needed to reach the gold ore. After the initial drilling, blasting and equipping of a mineshaft, tunnels are built leading outwards from the main shaft so that the gold reef can be reached. Shaft mining is a dangerous operation, and roof supports are needed so that the rock does not collapse. There are also problems of the intense heat and high pressure below the surface, which make shaft mining very complex, dangerous and expensive.

For every ton of ore that is mined, only a tiny amount of gold is ever extracted. Several methods can be used to separate the gold from its ore, but one of the more customary methods is called gold cyanidation when the ore is crushed and then a cyanide solution is added, and the gold particles are chemically dissolved and separated from the ore. The gold is therefore oxidised. Powdered zinc is then added to the cyanide solution. The zinc isolates the gold, so that the gold is quickly extracted out of the solution.

Gold has a lot of qualities and this is why it is a sought after commodity. It sparkles and shines; it is durable; it is flexible and can be bent and twisted in shape. It is valuable and a good conductor of electricity, so it is good for circuits and wires. Fire fighters use gold in their protective masks because gold is a heat reflector.

In the Bible, gold has always been associated with royalty, kings and Kingdoms. The first time the word, 'gold' appears in the Bible is in Genesis 2:11, 12:

> **"The name of the first is Pishon: that is it which compasseth the whole land of Havilah, where there is gold; And the gold of that land is good: there is bdellium and the onyx stone."**

In this context gold is used to reflect the affluence and splendour of Havilah, and currently, gold still reflects these things. To me, gold represents a precious product, valuable, and rare, but as we learnt, gold does have to go through a process before it is fit for purpose.

If you have ever observed gold mining, you will know that it is intense and gruelling. In my life, I have been through processes that have been like gold mining. Some of the progressions have not always been easy, but I have learnt from the experiences and become a better person. When gold is mined, it is accessed, broken, separated, extracted, purified and refined. After completion It is completely different to its raw state, and it reappears shining and beautiful. The gold always had its original qualities but it had to be processed for it to be suitable for use.

When one is pursuing a dream or vision, there will be times when you will feel crushed, drained, and even belittled, but we must go through the processes to be fit for purpose. The point is, that sometimes we will never know what we are capable of until we go through incidences that extract and display qualities that lay dormant within us.

To obtain a gold medal, athletes and sports people have to train, prepare, and push themselves beyond expectations. They go through a process and schedule to obtain their marked prize. Going for goal is a mark of excellence and it often takes strategy and process to achieve excellence. Let's learn from the gold mining experience and go for gold.

Reflections on August

August—
Augustus Caesar's Month

August was the sixth month in the Roman calendar and was called 'Sextillis'. In the days of Numa it had 29 days. The Roman Senate decided to name the month after Augustus Caesar, the Grand Nephew of Julius Caesar. The senate also decided to give it 31 days instead of 30, as they did not want anyone to think they had given Caesar's Grand Nephew an inferior month. The extra day was taken from February giving it 28 days and 29, in a leap year.

Augustus was a successful leader and to acknowledge his accomplishments the Senate named the month after him. One of his significant victories was that by his defeat of Anthony and Cleopatra, Rome regained its control of Egypt. This all took place in the month of August.

Augustus' victories put an end to several civil wars of the Roman empire, and the Senate declared that so far, it had been the most fortunate month for them. This justified further why the month should be named after Augustus. Augustus Caesar clarified and completed the calendar reform of his Grand Uncle Julius Caesar.

Incidentally, the Anglo Saxons called August *Weod Monath* which means' month of the weed.'

The Resilient Weed

August 1st-13th

Have you ever thought of how resilient some weeds are? August, as we know was called the weed month by the Anglo Saxons. I have certainly had my fair share of weed encounters in my garden and even in my grass, where I have had to root, dig up and pull out; and even when I have done this on a regular basis, certain weeds seem even more adamant that they are not moving.

The other day I had quite a fierce weed encounter: this weed was not only rooted very deeply, but it also had prickles! Imagine my disgust when I was not only scratched, but I was pricked as well! Every time there is a bout of rain, my garden seems to have a renewed weed epidemic, and everyone else in my household seems to be gardening shy, suffering from spade and fork aversion.

I have learnt a lot about weeds. They are resilient—they just keep coming back, even when they are cut, chopped, dug out, and burnt. They even have the ability to come back and reinvent themselves! Some of them have an excellent camouflage, looking beautiful among all the other flowers, and then you suddenly come to the realisation "I didn't plant this, how did it get there?

When times are hard, and things are tough, I think about the resilient weed and how it just keeps coming back no matter what has been applied to it. Sometimes they only way to get rid of the

weed is to use weed killer, and then you wip'
as well! Repeated weed epidemics, dare I s
to build up our resilience. Analogically, b
from all the digging, and the energy expended u, ɔ
actually quite healthy. Taking out my frustration on the resɪ.
weed is therapeutic. I am often reminded how I ought to be
in my challenging life encounters and that resilience is a key
component in the implementation of my dream and in seeing
out my vision.

Be resilient, keep going forward and do not be put off by early
failures.

"The Resilient Weed"

Prepare for Change
August 14th-21st

August is often considered to be a transitional month because it is the final month of summer. It is the time of year we begin to wind-down from our holiday travels and prepare for autumn. Whether we appreciate it or not, it is in fact a time of change. Change should be planned and prepared for so we may accommodate it appropriately.

Current theories around change emphasise that it is indeed a process with distinct phases. I agree because change as I have experienced it, does not constitute one single action. Prochaska, DiClemente and Norcross have created a very useful model, which outlines the stages of the change process. They are the following:

- Pre-Contemplation
    o A person is not even thinking about making a change

- Contemplation
    o A person has started thinking that making a change might be a good idea and is perhaps making plans about how to implement those changes

- Preparation / Action
  - o A person is taking concrete steps which will lead to changing their behaviour

- Maintenance
  - o A person maintains the change in the behaviour through continued effort

- Termination
  - o The change is now ingrained and the person no longer has to make great efforts to maintain the change

- Recycling
  - o A person returns from any given stage to an earlier stage.

To help yourself to adapt to change, it is useful to;

- Do w hat I call a change inventory, recording every aspect of the change
- Reflect on your values and consider whether your intended change reflect them
- Reconnect with your dream and vision, and be flexible and creative, keeping your options open
- Encourage and affirm yourself so you employ the correct mind-set
- Continue to be a visionary. This way you will see the bigger picture and not only issues that affect you directly

The best change is a planned change. Have a good one!

Have a Carnival before Autumn

August 22nd-31st

The Brazilian Carnival in Rio, Brazil, is an annual festival that takes place four days before Ash Wednesday, which is described as the beginning of the 40 days fast, called Lent. During the days of fasting, some Roman Catholics and other Christians do not consume meat. The Carnival is held to bid farewell to some pleasures of the flesh and it is dedicated to Christ's Death.

The Brazilian Carnival is a little different from its European counterparts because it is a fusion of European and African cultural practices. Although in Brazil there are slight regional differences in each city, the cultural fusion is evident in its music, rhythm and costumes worn by participants.

The modern carnival originated in the year 1641. It was actually mimicry of the European style of having fun. However, over the years, it reframed itself and took inputs from different cultures like Europe, North America and Africa.

Elements of the Caribbean carnival are also related to the 'carnevale', an Italian Catholic costume festival before the day of Lent. Similar to its Brazilian equivalent, the Caribbean carnival is also an example of many African festivals whose purpose is to cleanse, renew and revive the community by parading through villages in costumes and masks.

Caribbean carnivals need to be held in the community so there can be maximum participation. As the carnival travels through the towns, villages and districts, the music is said to cleanse the air, clearing cobwebs, dispelling the year's troubles. The vibrant costumes are supposed to clean your eyes so all see a brighter future. The friendly dancing people and joyous atmosphere supposedly banish bad feelings, creating new friendships and renewing old ones.

In Europe too, Festivals and rituals have frequently brought together communities for a common purpose. Festivals and rituals serve to unite communities for a common cause, allowing people to act frivolously and vent the emotions of everyday life, placing people of different social classes and genders on equal footing.

Why not arrange an event that will bring people together? You don't have to have your friends or colleagues parading in costumes. It would be like your own mini carnival where people of different cultures, ages, and classes may unite. This would be an ideal way to close summer bringing you into, and preparing you for, the autumnal season.

A unifying event is also a good way to get people to sign up to an idea. If you need to influence people regarding your dream or vision, then I would propose you arrange a unifying event. Happy celebrations!

Reflections on September

September—
The Seventh Month

According to the Georgian calendar, September is the ninth month and in the past, the month has had 29 and 31 days, but since the time of the emperor Augustus, it has had only 30 days. The Romans believed that September was overseen by the god, *Vulcan*, the god of 'fire and forge.' The Romans expected fires, volcano's, and earthquakes to occur in September because of this.

September originates from the Roman word **septem,** meaning 'seven,' because it was the seventh month of the Roman calendar. September was also known as **Gerst Monath** (Barley Month) to the Anglo Saxons as this was the time they harvested barley to make a special brew. They also called September, **Haefest Monath** or harvest month. Harvest time was important to the Anglo Saxons because they were very dependent on the land for food. After the harvest, there were rituals of thanksgiving, celebrating the yield of crop. The Harvest festival pre-dates Christian times in Britain. Anglo Saxon farmers offered their first grain to the goddess of fertility. They often sacrificed an animal, which represented the spirit of the grain in the hope that this spirit would continue to bring them good fortune for the continuity of good harvests.

It was not until 1843 that the Christian contexts of harvest celebration began. The Reverend Robert Hawker invited parishioners to a special thanksgiving service at his church at

Morwenstow in Cornwall. In Britain this led to the custom of decorating churches with local produce in September. Later on, many churches would not only give thanks to God, but, they would also give produce to those who were less fortunate in their communities.

The celebration of harvest continues today in Britain and for the most part this tradition is practised in September. In The USA and Canada harvest is celebrated later in the year, and is called thanksgiving. It also tends to be a more secular event although many churches and religions embrace it.

Nurturing your Seed
September 1st-20th

The parable of the Sower is one of Jesus' parables found in 3 of the Gospels in the Bible.

The story is about a sower that drops seeds, which fell on different types of soil. Some fell on rocky ground, some among thorns. Other seeds were lost, but when the seed fell on the good soil it grew and yielded a very healthy crop.

We have a responsibility to nurture our seeds. We all have seeds of greatness on the inside of us. When we are implementing a dream or vision we should nurture and cultivate our seeds, allowing our ideas to develop. We should discern the people we meet. Some people will help us on our pathway and aide our development, others may ridicule us, and tell us that our ideas will not work because they may be jealous, covet our abilities or just genuinely do not understand our perspectives. We must foster our seeds, and ensure our ideas are deposited on good soil; so we are not wasting our time sowing in the wrong area. You may have to part company with some people who have become a hindrance to what you want to do. This is fine; they may come back into your life at a later stage when you have both developed further.

I had an experience where one of my congregation members publicly rubbished my writing. I used to produce church newsletters and one day she said quite openly before the church congregation that she hadn't bothered to read the newsletter that I had distributed. She went on to say that furthermore, she had too many things to read at work and so she couldn't be bothered to read it. The newsletter was meant to be a tool of communication for church members. The newsletter could be emailed, posted or otherwise distributed, to congregants who could not always attend services. She completed her tirade of complaints by saying that my communication wasn't effective.

I discovered quite incidentally some time later, that she was criticising my work only because she had a desire to write herself and didn't feel able to do so.

We have to be careful and detect these situations, so that we do not replicate the same behaviour or belittle the person criticising you. Protect yourself from negativity by all means, nurturing your seed so that your ideas fall on good soil. However, always try and keep a good, pure and honest heart. This way, your seed will remain nurtured.

Seed Bearers
September 21st-30th

The phrase, "You will reap what you sow," is a deep statement reminding us how important it is to conduct ourselves appropriately. Good conduct is expressed throughout the Bible and the analogy about reaping and sowing is often used to this end. However, I would want to use this phrase in a slightly different context, and that is, to imagine yourself as a seed bearing plant.

Seed bearers are plants that have the ability to reproduce. The plants themselves may die, but their offspring are by-products of their seed. These seeds live on and are prolific, so the species is able to continue.

We should be like seed bearing plants, implanting goodness and kindness. Impacting the communities and areas where we live and far beyond. This is the legacy we should all desire to leave.

When you are implementing your dream and vision, particularly if it is something that is humanitarian that can be passed on to future generations, you'll need to succession plan, so that your product and the impact of your dream will continue prolifically. For your dream or vision to continue you will need to plant seeds as investments in others. In the parable of the Fig tree, in the Bible, Jesus curses the tree because it has been unproductive. The lesson here is that if we are to be productive, the fruits of our labour needs to be visible, and then shared and passed on to others allowing the beneficiaries to carry out what has been started.

Seeds are distributed by seed bearers who in turn are not afraid to share their gifts and insights throughout their lifetime.

Reflections on October

October—
The Eighth Month

October is the tenth month of the Julian and Gregorian calendars, but was the eighth month in the Roman calendar and retained its name from this period. Originating from the Latin word *octo,* meaning eight. October was introduced after January and February into the reformed calendar created by the Romans. It is one of seven months with a length of 31 days. In most years, January starts on the same day of the week as October, but no other month starts on the same day of the week as October in leap years.

Commonly associated with autumn in the northern hemisphere, October is the time of gathering fallen leaves. October is the time of spring in the southern hemisphere.

The Anglo-Saxon name for October is **Winterfylleth** which is said to be made up of two words, 'winter and full moon.' The Anglo Saxons divided the year into two seasons, winter and summer. The six months when the days were longer was summer, and the other six months with the shorter days was winter. Mid-October was said to be the beginning of the winter season. The period of two days when winter began was called **Veturnætur** ('meaning winter nights') and in pre—Christian Norse tradition, there were sacred rites of sacrifice and feasting in which each family participated.

Be on top of things so we can move forward
October 1st-14th

I am once again returning to my gardening theme and reflecting on what tasks I must do in October. In September we did have some warmer days but now October has begun, it has definitely become colder.

It has not been easy to continuously rake up fallen autumn leaves, but I have taken comfort in the fact that they provide a wonderful mulch that will nourish the soil in my garden. Fortunately, I have no climbing roses to prune. I think you must have gathered by now, that I am a rather reluctant gardener, so I look out for low maintenance plants and shrubs, but still, October is the month where certain tasks have to be carried out in preparation for the next season.

When we are following a dream or vision there may be tasks that have to be carried out periodically. I call them the maintenance jobs, which may appear menial because they are repetitive and mundane. Nevertheless, they are jobs that have to done because they are usually preparatory tasks which help us to move on to the next phase or season.

Clearing the leaves helps me to prepare the ground for the planting of my new spring seeds. If I didn't do this task regularly it would, firstly, leave me with too much to do at any one time. Secondly, my spring plants would lose out on having a nourished environment to grow and thrive in.

In following a dream or vision there may be administrative jobs that you need to do regularly. Try not to procrastinate; do the jobs habitually and systematically. This is a much better approach which will greatly inhibit things piling up. When you are faithful in the smaller tasks you will know you can be trusted with much bigger ones. Preparatory tasks help us to make much smoother transitions to the next phase or season. It is often the smaller and more mundane tasks that act as significant stepping stones in our implementation plan. In completing these tasks we will advance at a more even pace.

Protection from the Cold
October 15th-20th

October is the time, if you haven't already, to remove tender potted plants from the harsh conditions outside placing them in a more sheltered environment. Tender plants often don't fare well if they're taken directly indoors from the garden. The air inside the house is generally too dry and the temperatures too varied from what they are used to. The result can be dropped or damaged leaves.

What is needed is a transitional place for about a week on a sheltered patio or in an unheated greenhouse before they are put inside the house. You can help prepare the plants by cutting back on water in late summer, giving only enough to prevent wilting. The plants should be prepared in advance. Take the time to do this as the results are worth it. The bottom of the pots should be checked for slugs and pests because this is where they hide. These will need to be cleaned off so the plants may be trimmed.

There are two reasons for trimming plants. Firstly, they won't take up as much room, secondly, by trimming the plant, you are forcing it to produce new leaves and shoots. These will develop under indoor conditions and therefore will not have to go through a period of adjusting to the new environment, as the plants will already be acclimatised. Trimming the plant also lessens the effects on old foliage, which was produced outside, causing less of a fall out when it reacts to the new environment by leaves turning yellow and falling off. Winter flowering plants should not be trimmed. All this done, the plants are ready for their transfer inside.

We transfer tender plants indoors so they are not exposed to the elements. We protect them so they may survive and endure another season or year. So it is with ourselves: there are times we need to protect our vision and dream from the external cold. This can mean many things to us, it may represent misunderstandings and misinterpretation. It can mean ridicule, criticism, disrespect, or even discrimination.In these circumstances we need to protect our dreams and visions. Here are five tips, which can help you to do this:

- Some dreams or visions are not made for sharing or should only be revealed at a specific time. Make sure you share your vision at an appropriate time.
- If you are sharing your vision or dream, make sure it is with like-minded people who will not discourage you, particularly if they don't understand your intentions.
- Keep your dream or vision alive by nurturing it with information, and associating yourself with like-minded people.
- Keep good records. You may need to prove copyright or ownership, obtain licences, patents, or planning permission. Record and date things, and obtain advice where necessary.
- Stick to your plan and make the adjustments where necessary and cultivate an environment that will help you to grow.

- Follow and develop you inner-voice so in the times when you have to go it alone you will have the ability to encourage yourself.

Finally, let me end with an old English proverb "A vision without a plan is just a dream. A plan without a vision is just drudgery. But a vision with a plan can change the world." Protect your dream and vision.

Harvesting your fruit
October 21st-31st

I have grown a number of fruits and vegetables over the years and I have found home-grown vegetables and fruit taste much better than those available in the supermarkets, but to be at their best, fruits need to be harvested at the right time.

In the past, I made the mistake of leaving fruits on the tree and bushes too long; they rotted, got invaded with pests or became really fibrous and tough, not good at all.

It is important to harvest at the right time so the fruit will be in its prime, giving optimum taste and value. When I have harvested the fruit I preserve the fruit in several ways, making jams and chutneys, putting them in liqueurs, making pies and puddings and even making ciders, perries and wines. "The better the fruit, the better the product".

Doing things at the correct time is important or it can have adverse effects, causing us to waste time and resources and resulting in frustration. When we are following our dreams it is easy to become frustrated so we should try and work to a plan as much as possible, project managing our tasks is a good way, to ensure things get done on time, so we don't overstretch ourselves and loose heart. When we harvest correctly we are indeed giving ourselves a mark of excellence a formidable tool for marketing ourselves.

Reflections on November

November—
The Ninth Month

The word November derives from the Latin word *novem*, meaning 'nine' because originally it was the ninth month in the Roman calendar. It became the eleventh month of the year after the order was changed in 1582 when countries adopted the Gregorian calendar.

The Anglo Saxons called November *Blotmonað*, ('month of blood sacrifices') and the Icelandic word has a similar meaning.

Gormánuáðr or 'gor-month' meaning 'slaughtering-month,' November was usually the time of year when livestock that was not expected to survive the winter would be slaughtered and used for meat. There would be rituals and ceremonies surrounding the butchering, and offerings would be made to the gods.

This tradition was common practice in most parts of Northern Europe.

Sacrifices
November 1st-20th

I started my working career in childcare and then graduated to social work and teaching. For many years I worked in the area of Equality and Diversity. In Social Work there were many families from minority ethnic groups who were in the hard end of what we now call safeguarding; with many children ending up in the care system. Concurrently, I was always very active in my church and became an ordained minister of religion and practised a successful ministry over the last thirty years.

My life at times has been an uphill struggle as I have found myself in very political roles; in the hub of addressing injustice and disadvantage. In Anglo Saxon times November was known as **Blotmonað,** (month of blood sacrifices). You may now be wondering why I am making these connections. Well, throughout Judaic Christianity we see parallels of blood sacrifices, and blood still remains a key component in the understanding of Christian sacrifice generally. Jesus' crucifixion is regarded by Christians as the "perfect sacrifice". When you are in political roles like the ones I refer to, you are constantly fighting against injustices and sacrifices are often made at a detriment to yourself. You pave the way for others to progress because of the battles you have fought. They are then able to move forward by standing on the shoulders of those who have gone before them.

The church I grew up in refused to ordain women for many years. I realised from quite an early age, that I had a vocation in church ministry. I left my original church, and the one to which I went recognised my vocation and I was trained quite intensively for church ministry. My training Minister was a pioneer of women's ministry and in one way he was exceptionally hard on me because he wanted me to be successful. He was ridiculed, ostracised, and harshly criticised for training women and many of his counterparts refused to associate with him. However, he persevered and as a consequence, he ordained both male and female ministers who later became most successful in their fields.

There were also pioneering women along with myself, who sacrificed their reputations to stand up for what they believed in. I am grateful to the people who went before me, like the late Reverend I. O. smith, who worked tirelessly in the area of women's ministry in Britain and the Caribbean enduring criticism and unpopularity, fighting for what she believed in. She paved the way for women like myself to be in ministry today.

I am a keen viewer of the drama 'Dr Quinne Medicine Woman' played by the actress Jane Seymour. It is about the trials and adventures of a female doctor in a small wild western USAtown. The programme focuses on Dr. Mike, a woman doctor in a time when it was unheard of. The prejudices and discrimination faced by female doctors and women at the time is accurately depicted. It starts with her journey to Colorado Springs to be the town's physician after her father's death in 1868. Each episode portrays a different struggle and how she overcomes.

An episode that comes to mind is when Dr Quinne opens the town's first library. Because of ignorance the people burn the books as they felt that some of the books were promoting heresy. Eventually, the town's people come round, but it is at a cost to Dr Mike as most of the books given to her by her late father were destroyed. It is evident, according to the programme, that Dr Quinne sacrificed an upper class life style in Boston for a difficult and challenging one as a country female doctor in Colorado Springs. She was ridiculed, misunderstood, criticised, opposed, but her character exhibits commitment, faithfulness and tenacity—qualities that I admire in anyone.

Subsequently, I learnt that on November 1, 1848—The first medical school for women opened in Boston. The Boston Female Medical School was founded by Samuel Gregory with just twelve students. In 1874, the school merged with the Boston University School of Medicine, becoming one of the first co-ed medical schools. Many women and men faced opposition and made great sacrifices for this to happen. To get to where you want to be you will need to make sacrifices. Not everyone will understand your dream or vision and sometimes when you are pioneering you will undoubtedly be misunderstood. I can only encourage you to hold on, because at least you will have paved the way for others and you will leave a legacy for the next generation.

The month of November is known for a number of things, here are but a few:

- November 1, 1993—The European Union came into existence as a result of the Maastricht Treaty.

- November 1, 1995—The first all-race local government elections took place in South Africa, marking the end of the apartheid system.
- November 7, 1989—L. Douglas Wilder became the first African American governor in U.S. history, elected governor of Virginia.
- November 7, 1990—Mary Robinson became Ireland's first female president.

Success is never without sacrifice so prepare yourself to succeed by building your broad shoulders and growing a thick skin. Sometimes, "the depth of our sacrifice indicates the height of our success".

The Art of Preservation
Make sacrifices without becoming the sacrificial lamb
November 21st[th]-30th

Food preservation is the process of treating and handling food to stop or slow down food spoilage. It usually involves preventing the growth of bacteria, fungi (such as yeasts), and other micro-organisms as well as retarding the oxidation of fats which cause rancidity which lead to a loss of quality, edibility, or nutritional value. I have used several methods of food preservation in my time, preserving fruit by turning it into jam, salting or drying meat and fish or by curing. Many processes designed to preserve food will involve a number of food preservation methods.

In November, the Anglo Saxons slaughtered the animals that they thought would not make it through their cold winters. They killed the animals and preserved the meat, so they would have adequate food for their families throughout the long winter months. The Anglo Saxons also made sacrifices to their Deities and there were many rituals and ceremonies surrounding the butchering. A prized animal would be selected as the sacrifice, and then be butchered and given for appeasement to the gods. In some cultures this is called scapegoating when an animal is selected to represent the sin and wrong-doings of a community and symbolically put out of the community or slaughtered.

Scapegoating, if we for a moment take it out of its analogical context, is a serious and dysfunctional problem with one member of a social group being blamed for things, picked on and constantly denigrated. It is a projection defence. It is the ego saying "If I can put the blame on you, I don't have to recognize and take responsibility for the negative qualities in myself. What I can't stand about myself, I really hate in you and have to attack you for it in order to deny that I have the same quality." It is a discrediting routine by which people blame and move responsibility away from themselves and towards a targeted person or group. It is also a practice by which angry feelings and hostilities are vented.

When you are implementing a dream or vision, you have to carefully strategize and equip yourself so that you develop courage and tenacity. During times of adversity it is easy to become scapegoated and targeted particularly if you are trying to pioneer something new, or implementing change. It is important that you understand that people may try to scapegoat you, particularly, if they do not understand what you are about. Adopt strategies that will preserve your integrity. Ensure you have your support networks in place and you know who your allies are. If you need to learn something new make sure you do, as it will reduce your vulnerability.

When you are following your dream or vision you will inevitably have to make sacrifices, but you really do not have to be the scapegoat or sacrificial lamb.

Reflections on December

December—
the tenth month

December used to be the tenth month of the year in the Roman calendar. The month gets its name from the word *decem* meaning 'ten'. December had 30 days, until Numa when it had 29 days, and then with Julius Ceasarwhen it became 31 days long.

December marked the beginning of winter in the northern hemisphere and was usually a time of snow, rain and wind. In Roman history, Saturnalia was a festival originally held on December 17th. Later, the celebrations expanded with unofficial festivities held right through to the 23rd December.

Saturnalia was celebrated with a sacrifice at the temple of Saturn in the Roman forum and public banquet; followed by private and continuous gift-giving and endless partying. This carnival like atmosphere overturned traditional social norms. Gambling was permitted, and it was the turn of masters to serve their slaves.

According to Roman mythology, Saturn was said to be an agricultural deity who reigned over the world in the golden age. The inflections of Saturnalia were supposed to mimic conditions of the lost mythical age. The Greek equivalent was Kronia. The popularity of Saturnalia continued into the 3rd and 4th centuries AD, and as the Roman Empire came under Christian rule, most of its contents diminished, but, some of the residue customs have influenced some seasonal celebrations linked to Christmas and the New Year. This is particularly true of British celebrations.

The Anglo Saxons called December *Winter Monath* or *Yule Monath* because of the custom of burning of the Yule log to celebrate the next most significant festival in December, Winter Solstice. The coming of winter was celebrated by families and was traditionally the time when farmers and fishermen gathered food in preparation for the coming cold season. It was also a time for family reunions.

Like Saturnalia, traces of this ancient festival may be linked to modern Christmas celebrations and the yule log is evidence of this in Britain. Many Anglo Saxons converted to Christianity, and the new converts called December *Heligh Monath*, or *Holy Month.* December became the month when the birth of Jesus was celebrated.

No present Under the Christmas Tree
December 1st-20th

I have always visualised myself as a generous person, particularly to family and friends; always giving my time and energy to good causes.

I remember several Christmases ago when the entire family gathered around our pretty and well-decorated tree after our festive dinner. I had gone out of my way to ensure the family were accommodated. I bought presents for the children who were young, both under eight years old, and for my partner. I baked cakes and gave them as gifts to in-laws and friends. We were on a tight budget, you see; nevertheless I had found ways to give.

We all sat down to open our presents and I passed each person his gift, until nothing was left under the tree. Then, it suddenly hit me: there was no present for me under the Christmas tree. No one had bought me a present. Yes, I had been invited to dinner and we had visited family and friends and they had wished us well for the season. The point still remained that there was no present for me to unwrap. I cleared up all the wrapping paper and emptied it in the waste bin. I sat down and poured myself a well-deserved glass of wine.

I had worked hard that Christmas serving my family well, I thought. I had always believed Christmas to be a time of sharing and giving, replicating the Christian values of kindness and love. It is really hard when you feel you have given, loved and yet you don't appear to receive anything back for yourself. I consoled myself with the fact that you don't give to receive. However, I was of the belief that encouragement sweetens our labour.

I learnt an important lesson that Christmas: in order to love others you must love yourself. I discovered that one of the ways I show love to others is by giving gifts. I had served others so faithfully, but had neglected to communicate my own needs. I had set a barometer of neglect and one of the manifestations of this was no present under the Christmas tree for me.

You should never serve others at the expense of neglecting yourself. You will inevitably burn yourself out. Since that Christmas, I have looked after myself as well as serving others. When I buy Christmas presents now, I always buy one for myself. It is a way of valuing and appreciating me. Let my lesson be a lesson to us all: you can love and serve others, but we must learn to love and care for ourselves in the process. If we feel cared for and our internal self-love is nurtured, we will love others more genuinely.

Celebrate

December 21st-31st

Once in a while, it's important to stop, reflect and think about your accomplishments before you move on to the next activity or phase of implementing your dream or vision. No matter how small it is, reaching a milestone is worth celebrating. We are used to celebrating things like baptism, confirmation or other religious milestones depending on our faith. We celebrate weddings, moving to new homes, birthdays and a whole host of other things. Celebrating our achievements helps us to have new meaning to life and gives us personal encouragement, which contributes to our health and wellbeing.

The other day I celebrated an important milestone. I had set myself a savings target for the year. I reached this milestone in the month of October, two months earlier than expected. It was an important milestone as over the years I had had to address debts that I had built up from being a single parent: I also had a house that needed constant repairs. This year I cleared one significant debt and another substantial loan. Surely these achievements were worth celebrating?

I didn't go over-board; but a friend who knew about my struggles had lunch with me. She congratulated and encouraged me to reach further goals and we celebrated my achievements together.

When we are implementing our vision and working at our dreams we have to find ways of encouraging ourselves. One of the ways we can do this is to celebrate our mile-stones. It helps to record them so you can look back at them. They will provide you with a source of fulfilment and at a later stage you can say to yourself, actually, I am not doing so badly after all.

Poems
& Verses

Carry Me

Carry me to a place of warmth and peace;
Where I will rest my weary hear on your shoulders of quietness.
The echelons of love portrayed when you firmly embrace
And take me into your contented domain.
Carry me!

Carry me to the heavenly place of blessed tranquillity
Where you steal my apathy and give me divine care;
And lead me to a dwelling of rich generosity.
Carry me!

Carry me to the highest heights and sincere depths
Of your inmost heart, so I may live and sustain
Your dialogue of mercy of and love.
Carry me!
Carry me to your secret place wherein I can hold your heart
Deepest heart.
Carry me!

Don't You Understand?

Don't you understand that I am not after material gain?
Houses, land, cars and things which only satisfy for a moment.
Don't you understand that although I am grateful for the gifts you lavish on me, five minutes of your undivided attention is worth more than a life time of whimsical presents.
Don't you understand that more than pearls, diamonds, rubies, gold and silver, or any precious jewels, you to me are far more valuable. And all the time in the world is not long enough for me to be in your company.
Don't you understand that a walk with you in the countryside or by the sea; hearing your words of strength, or being held in your strong arms of love is worth more riches than a thousand kingdoms.
Don't you understand?
What is it that you don't understand about the deep and unwavering love I have for you?

How Can I Express?

How can I express the depth of joy I feel?
When I see words that come from you on a page
In a text or in a letter;
Words that are heart felt and so clear.

How can I express the peace and tranquillity I feel?
Knowing I can be secure in you and your love is expressed far
and near;
From a distant shore and so much more and you say
I miss you and long to see you.

How can I express that when you say,
Those words I long to hear, I love you.
I'm overwhelmed because I really love you too.

How Lovely

How lovely is the morning when I awake
And my thoughts are centred on you.
You are compared to the sunrise
That ascends; shining, bringing warmth and light
At the start of my day.

How lovely is the noontide as my hunger is filled
With laughter and joy, igniting my soul.
Grounding me for what lies ahead.
Strengthening my mind and raising my spirit
In the midmost of my day.

How lovely are the intimate moments shared with you:
Your tender touch, fondness, carrying me to heights of love.
A journey of reflection giving inner joy and peace
In the midst of my twilight day.

How lovely is the fervent, undeniable, unique love you bestow
and shower on me.

How Wonderful

How wonderful is the love,
That rises in the morning.

It does not set or go down at Eventide.
But is ever shining through the darkness.

Unreserved love is the light and substance of life.
And so is the love I have for you my darling;
Limitless, unrestricted and bounteous.
I Love you unconditionally.

I Found You

I found you on that day when I travelled distantly.
Fatigued I entered the room. You were there, but, at first I didn't notice you across the way. I seated myself nervously not knowing what to expect in this new environment. I was anxious yet eager to learn.
I found you on that day we worked tirelessly together and with others debating, searching for answers analysing each case with precision, to not miss the point or misconstrue any idea raised.
I found you on that day so stimulating, exploring my mind and questioning my every response, clarifying every comment.
And restating for all to understand, so all could learn and appreciate what was being said.
I found you on that day when your eyes connected with my soul and I saw into your spirit that you wanted me to be more than just an ordinary friend. Your acts of continued tenderness and display of momentary gestures and glances making me feel so special.

I found you on that day; and you found my heart!

I Haven't Heard

I haven't heard from you for some time now,
And how my heart aches for your voice.
I had noticed that your calls have become infrequent,
And your notes hurried with fewer words.
Your silence speaks volumes to me though,
And your lack of contact leads me to contemplate
Why your interest in me has diminished so rapidly.
I have reflected on whether I ever occupied a place in your life.
It is painful to even consider myself to you as a passing whim.
Do I possess nothing that you could at least extract for friendship?
Friends to me are for life; But then, they need to be true.
Is it that I have offended you unawares or there is something
within me that you dislike so intensely that you find it difficult
to put into words.
It would have aided my development and help me to grow as a
human being; at least.
The truth spoken in love does less harm, than punitive silence in
dismay.
But your silence does speak, it tells me I no longer have a place
in your heart!

I Miss You

I miss you and your voice that speaks so deeply of the stories of adventure and experience.
I miss you with your warmth, zest for life, company, countenance, and pleasure.
I miss you for your strength, security, and interest that show in me.
I miss you for your enclosed comfort and signature of compassion displayed on me.

I miss you and your eyes of charity, intensely observing, yet energising me.
But most of all, I miss you and your heart of love that you felt free enough to display and give to me.

I Receive

I receive from your fountain of refreshing kindness.
I receive from your river of ever increasing joy.
I receive from your sea of redemptive laughter.
I receive from your ocean of delivering strength.

I receive the purity of your honest affection.
I receive from the covenant of your gracious help.
I receive from your grace amidst all my conflict.
I receive your vision and zest for life.

I receive from your testimony of goodness.
I receive from your favour and strengthening faith.
I receive from your wealth and overwhelming promise.
I receive the essence of your sanctifying love.

I Sang Today My Love

I sang today my love as I thought about you.
A song of words that were heart felt
And backed by heavenly music.

I sang today my love and I visualised a choir singing with me.
Captivated by the melodious harmony,
A symphony to all ears.

I sang today my love with an orchestra of amazing instruments.
Woodwind, brass, percussion and stringed.
Bringing joy and happiness to all the hearers.

I sang today my love but my imagination ran away
with me.
Guess What? My only audience was you!

I Saw You

I saw you and noticed,
A figure of manliness advancing towards me,
Leaving imprints of authority and presence.
Commanding as you interacted and spoke,
Liaising with all around.

I saw you and discerned you.
Mindful of your display of intellect.
Ability far beyond your years.
Words chosen precisely yet discreetly,
A gifted spirit, portraying many desirable gifts.

I saw you and received you.
Your kindness and charitable persona.
Your handsome and well defined appearance.
Igniting much buried passions,
Bringing untold joy to my eyes.

I saw you and needed you.
And now you have become the unbridled love of my life.

I Was Only Thinking Of You

I was only thinking of you when I arranged for you to meet all those people to enhance your prospects and improve your plans. I was only being a friend and sister, I am faithful like that.

I was only thinking of you when I planned that business engagement. I recognised you as a leader in your field, and wanted your talents and outstanding abilities to be seen by others; for you to role model a new generation. I'm loyal like that!

I was only thinking of you when I arranged for you and your friends to attend that award winning dinner, where all the top aristocrats were attending, leaders, and trendsetters were honoured, I'm committed like that!
I was only thinking of you but don't worry I only wanted to give something back that I mistakenly thought you were giving to me!

I Wear a Crown

I wear a crown carved, shaped, especially for me.
Worn with dignity, decorated with copious jewels
My crown sparkles and shines.

My crown can be seen for miles around.
Transported by grace, fuelled by generosity.
Illuminating darkest of places.
Making peace where there is no justice.
My crown cries.

I wear a crown engraved with mercy.
Bearing marks of compassion and wit.
A sign of redeeming love.

My head held high as I wear my crown of majesty.
My crown smiles.
I wear a crown, which can only be described as a crown of
unconditional love.

Just to Hear You

Just to hear you.
Just a whisper or a faint sound
Of loving kindness and inspiration.
To know you are still oozing with love for me.
And the name that is pronounced from your lips
In sleep and wake is mine.
Just to hear you!

Just to hear you
And the sound of your influential voice.
Satisfying my emotions with peace,
Reassuring my security.
Knowing that my heart belongs to you and yours is mine.
Just to hear you!
Just to hear you.
Waking each fibre of my body.
Igniting passions of unconditional love, erasing the sleep of my
procrastination,
Resurrecting encouragement and truth.
Just to hear you ! Just to hear you.
Just for you to call my name in the morning.
Call my name at noon, and call my name at night.
So the deep sound of our penetrating voice
Will profoundly speak to my soul and resonate with my spirit.
Just to hear you, just to hear you my darling. Just to hear you
and your voice of love.

Love Ascends

Love ascends and rises far beyond any mountain peak;
Reaching above and beyond the clouds beyond the planets.
Not once, not twice, but thrice, ascending into the heavens,
And rising still exceeding unimaginable heights.

Love ascends exhaling refreshing invigorating winds of gladness
Revealing the ointment and fragrances of grace,
Calming sorrows, relieving pain, bringing comfort,
With the warmth of genuine affection and the power to inwardly
heal.

Love ascends and transcends my blood filled heart.
Soothing my soul, nurturing my spirit, reaching me,
Loving me, growing me and seeing me,
Enlightening me to renewed life: reframing the old recreating
me anew.
Love ascends all.

My Gift

My gift is a most wonderful acquisition.
Rich and fair, bold and kind'. Strikingly generous.
A pearl of humanity.
My gift is more precious to me than gold, silver, or any valuable
element this world could ever produce.
Minted and mined with greatness, intelligence, and purity
An iconic emergence of majesty and grace.
My gift contains attributes of honour and wit,
Gentlemanly prowess displayed with wisdom and charm.
Revealing friendship and truth
Standing up to the test of our time.
My gift unwraps pure, unadulterated affection
Feeding my soul, nurturing my spirit,
Quenching the hunger and thirst of my body
Awaking passions delivering joy to my very being
My gift is a divine revelation of unfaltering love.
Something I have never had before.
I am therefore grateful for the precious gift I have found in you!

My Man

My man calls me beautiful,
And he lays awake in the small hours
just to watch me sleep.
He's not afraid to hold my hand openly,
Or to hug me when he is with his friends.
He's my man.
My man always affirms me.
He thinks I'm lovable with or without my makeup.
And compliments me whether I am casual
or dressed up.
He acknowledges me when we are out in public
And compliments me when we are at home together alone.
That's my man.
My man says I am precious.

He compares me to rubies, diamonds, and precious stones,
Confessing that I am far more valuable to him than any material
thing.
I am his blessing and he cannot imagine life without me
My loving man.
My man says I am the best thing that's ever happened to him.
He loves me because he knows that I am his gift, given from above.

Reluctantly

Reluctantly I told you about the feelings I had developed for you. It took courage that day to tell you how I actually felt. I only did so knowing that the next day we would be going our separate ways, hundreds of miles and I wanted so much, for you not to walk out of my life; so on that final night of dare, I plucked up all the courage I could muster to say that I was truly and sincerely attracted to you.

I was socialised into being a good little Christian. A proper lady should not take the lead on issues of the heart, let alone tell a man you were interested in him. Hmmm, certainly not the done thing. You didn't seem to mind, though, only, that you misinterpreted my feelings in the belief that all I required from you was base and fervent lust. In fact you couldn't fathom the thought that all I wanted from you was your love and attention, nothing more.

My offer of good sacred love was therefore tinged by that accusation and triviality. Lust being the temporary measure it is, was not part of my consciousness and I failed miserably at hypocritically indulging in an activity that should have taken place in a different context. What I actually felt was love and my inexperience of one off momentary acts of passion got the better of me and that failed attempt to demonstrate I fear jeopardised my chance with you.

I must never again place myself in such a position of compromise making pure love suffer. Now to compensate I must ensure that the love I tried to initiate I must re-kindle from distant shores, and hope your interest will stand the test of time.

The moral of this story is that true love should never be demonstrated by lust.

Speak!

Speak and your words will reach me.
Speak and you words will teach me.
Speak and your words will enrich my soul.

Speak and your words will encase me.
Speak and your words will embrace me.
Speak and my body and spirit will be clothed in your love.

The Closer I Get

The closer I get to you I uncover your jewels of honesty hope and kindness. The veil of your heart being removed has left nothing but pleasurable uplifting, elevating me to heights of attainment inspiring my throbbing heart.

The closer I get to you I discover new treasures daily unearthed, as you choose to share your private aspirations, birthing new ideas, releasing self-worth, valuing my contributions, bringing out creativity and skill.

The closer I get to you I gain strength from your countenance of encouragement and your sunlit smile brings me joy in times of stress and worry, and you wrap me in your blanket of peace.

The closer I get to you I benefit from an intimacy and joy never experienced before, knowing that you care and you are willing to share your life with me.

The closer I get to you I feel love of the purest kind.
This kind of love spoken or untold brings out the best in me for you!

The Desire of my Heart

The desire of my heart is to be with you.
In your company, to hear your voice,
Locked in intimacy with you,
Held and sheltered by your body of love.

The desire of my heart is to see you face to face,
Beholding your nature of compassion,
Benefitting from your countenance of kindness,
Directed by your wisdom, and pathway of Gladness.

The desire of my heart is to be one with you,
Being of single mind to focus on the measures of purest poignant
love!
Reaching out with integrity,
Enclosed in your protective arms of authority.

The desire of my heart is to live to love you unconditionally, with
no regret on my part.

When You Spoke to Me

I don't know if you realised the affect you had when you spoke directly to me that day. I was new to the environment, one which you were already familiar with, so you unwittingly had me at a disadvantage. As I entered the room I tried really hard to inconspicuously seat myself. I ended up in your company, working with you that day

I was shocked, surprised and I didn't know where to put my face. Watt a ting! I could feel the blood rushing to my head. My face changed colour; it's rather shameful that my milk chocolate skin should be tinged with blood red. And my tingling body, the sweating, and you looked me straight in the eye and asked me that question.

My, I was so hot. I had to compose myself. I started fiddling with my hair, looked up down everywhere apart from your face. You were so gentlemanly yet direct. I suppose part of my amazement was that I actually felt valued by you. You were asking me what you should do and invited me to articulate my expectations. You were consciously genuine too. My word, I thought how did I ever get in this predicament of manifested blushing? You know what? I tried to style it out you know.

By trying to prolong and divert the conversation. But that didn't work; you brought it right back to me!

That was the day you reached my spirit and from ever since you have been in my heart!

You are so beautiful

Your poise and delightful countenance is a joy to all.
Your laughter, your smile ignites freshness and grace to a community,
Your words speak wisdom and communicate peace to a thousand nations.
You are so beautiful.

Your eyes bring light to many dark situations.
Your hair shines and sparkles in the dead and heat of the night.
Your face is a picture of compassionate and undiluted loving.
Your arms Bring solace to an uncomforted and grieving mind.
You are so Beautiful.

Your arms outstretch to the poor, needy, disadvantaged
Your feet travel to many distant lands
Meeting needs, sharing gifts, revealing your nature.
You are so beautiful.
Yes you are, oh so beautiful!

You Must Ascend

You must ascend!
To attain heights and beyond, move to places
where you will accomplish feats and thrive.
You must ascend!

You must ascend!
To exercise your gifts and talents,
Claiming your right to honour, fulfilling your destiny of greatness.
You must ascend!

You must ascend!
Upwards beyond your imagined calling,
Transcending limiting boundaries, c conquering, victorious.
You must ascend!

You must ascend !
Carried above by wings of love.
And as your ascent is built, on your spirit of truth,
You will soar and fly fuelled by potent love.
You must ascend!
You must and will ascend on the strength of my grace and
enriching affection.
I love you, Ascend you must!

Your eyes of Love

Your eyes of love reached me my darling.
The hope of renewed love that came from those piercing eyes,
Of truth looking into my every move, watching me,
Igniting healthy passion once again.

Your eyes of love persuasive, attentive, embracive,
Coaxing me to love again,
Reaching me and healing me,
Regenerating my affections.

Your eyes of love, fearless, expressive, impressive,
With a focus on positive intention,
Calling me, asking me,
To be the love of your life.

Your Heart of Gold

I love you my darling because of your wit and zest for life.
I love you! You are the kindest and considerate man I have ever
known.
Your generosity and gifts uplift you.
So humble but yet you are crowned with charity,
Embroidered with fine raiment of the heart
You hold your own and glow,

Gleaming bright you sparkle and shine.
You, my darling, are my leading light.
Bringing cheer to my darkest nights
Your heart displaying purity
That is second to none,
Tried and tested your heart undeniably of purest gold.

Your Heart Possession

You possess a heart that compares to none
Contents which shine beaming like the sun
Bright, yet true, precious, pure, refined.
You possess a heart won over by mine.

Your heart of love transparent and clear
Depicts kindness complete, and blessings to share
Mercy, enriching, compassion and grace
Energising, encouraging, declaring your faith.

Your heart of wisdom a treasure defined,
Patient, committed, a giver of time,
Lovingly discreet, you serve all my needs
My source, my help, a true friend indeed.

Your humour, your wit, transcends my core,
Awaking my spirit, countenance restored.
Passionate and faithful your love is bestowed
Enamoured so gracefully my heart is procured.

Quotes

A man without the heart to love
Will live a fruitless life.

But a man with a heart of love,

Will be fruitful and strong enough to
fulfil his passion and destiny.

Bank all your compliments,

So when you are alone and short
of self-esteem,

You can transfer credits to your
emotional account.

Love comes to us wrapped and
parcelled in different ways

But to gain the most benefit . . .

You should unwrap your gift slowly
to learn and utilise the package as
well as the gift!

Love is like a mirror reflected

You must give love and your loving
actions

Will be reflected throughout your
life.

Pure unadulterated love is like an
oasis to a man in a desert.

Respect is earned just like a
woman's love and then it must be
nurtured and maintained.

The choice to love is an investment
worth making,

As it pays dividends to all
concerned and promotes the
qualities of the giver.

The Fervent Love

"The Fervent unquenchable love of
a virtuous woman

Will quiet the heart of a wounded soul."

The True Light of Love

The true light of love illuminates the
darkest of souls and reignites the
passion of their humanity.

The Oasis of Love

The Oasis of true love
Quenches the thirst of a dry and
lonely soul.

The Waters of True Love

The waters of true love run deep
But the shallow waters of
infatuation will drown you in sorrow.

The well of overwhelming love

The well of overwhelming love
springs up into an everlasting
fountain of immeasurable
goodness and purity.

To Love Oneself

To love one's self appropriately
undeniably empowers one to love
another.

True Love

True love stands the test of time

But lust lasts a mere fleeting
moment.

True Men

True men value true women

True women value true men

And they will both realise they
deserve each other.

When we innately hate ourselves
The imperfections in others
become foremost

But as we love ourselves
It is easier to discover the hidden
treasure in all.

Lightning Source UK Ltd.
Milton Keynes UK
UKOW05f1918191113

221430UK00001B/25/P